The following volumes have been published in this series:

Herbert Haag

Theoretical Foundation of Sport Science as a Scientific Discipline

Contribution to a Philosophy (Meta-Theory) of Sport Science

VERLAG KARL HOFMANN D-73614 SCHORNDORF

Die Deutsche Bibliothek — CIP-Einheitsaufnahme

Haag, Herbert:
Theoretical foundation of sport science as a scientific discipline :
contribution to a philosophy (meta-theory) of sport science /
Herbert Haag. — 1. ed. — Schorndorf : Hofmann, 1994
  (Sport science studies ; Vol. 6)
  ISBN 3-7780-6461-4
NE: GT

Order Number 6461

© 1994 by Verlag Karl Hofmann, Schorndorf, Federal Republic of Germany

1st edition 1994

Total production: Karl Hofmann GmbH & Co., D-73614 Schorndorf, Federal Republic of Germany
Printed in Germany · ISBN 3-7780-6461-4

Table of Contents

List of Figures

List of Tables

Preface

The world of science is in constant development due to the change of sozial conditions as an external factor and the change of science itself as an internal factor. As part of this development new scientific questions and topics arise, which are initially dealt with by existing scientific disciplines. If these questions and topics represent an area which constantly gains importance, then new scientific disciplines emerge. They can be called theme-oriented or subject orientied scientific fields, since they have a theme or topic of high social relevanceas as ther body of knowledge. Examples for such themes or topics are: Information, work, nutrition, environment, but also movement, play, and sport.

The long established scientific fields such as philosophy, law, medicine, mathematics, physics etc. can be called discipline-oriented fields; from which knowledge is integrated in the theme-oriented scientific fields. This is one specific characteristic of so called theme-oriented sciences like sport science, in addition to the fact, that they have a shorter history than the discipline-oriented scientific fields.

Thus, it is necessary especially for these young sciences like sport science to establish theoretical foundations as a scientific discipline, to develop a meta-theory. This analysis attempts to make a contribution in this direction. It will be realized in the following steps.

"Introductory considerations" contain the logistics for this analysis, which means that first of all the purpose and the procedure of the investigation are clarified and described. In order to gain a better understanding central terms are defined. Clear terminology is of utmost importance, especially if the scientific dimensions of a given scientific field are examined. Finally, a short review of literature establishes a framework for the presented investigation.

These introductory considerations describe the meta-theory of sport science, the main focus of this analysis. This **meta-theory** comprises **four basic questions:**

— What is the aim and objective of sport science?
— What is the body of knowledge of sport science?
— What is the research methodology of sport science?
— What is the mutual relationship between theory and practice in sport science?

These four questions are constitutive for a meta-theory in general and for the attempt to describe the self-understanding of a scientific field in specific, in this case of sport science. Within the four central chapters of this analysis the attempt is made to formulate an answer to these four questions. Within each main chapter "preconsiderations (input)" **(Introduction)** are given at the beginning and "postconsiderations (output)" **(Conclusion)** conclude the chapter.

Section 1 deals with **"aims and objectives of sport science"** or with the question **"what is function of sport science"**? This is an extremely normative aspect, which is important for the perception of the scientific field. Four different dimensions will be analyzed in regard to this question, in order to give a comprehensive and well-balanced answer. The historical dimension can give an insight under generic perspectives. The comparative dimension may generate interesting facts due to a socio-cultural comparison across different nations. The status quo or present-day dimension relates to the current situation and a futuristic dimension can provide some perspectives for the future.

Section 2 deals with **"the body of knowledge of sport science"** or with the question **"what is the content of sport science"**? This question is fundamental for the understanding of a scientific field. There are many possibilities for describing and organizing the body of knowledge of sport science. A model comprising theory fields and subject fields of sport science will be presented in detail. With this model a dual approach towards the understanding of sport science is used, namely theory field - and subject-field-orientation, which is necessary to get a comprehensive view of the body of knowledge of sport science.

Section 3 deals with **"research methodology in sport science"** or with the question **"what is the process of gaining scientific knowledge in sport science"**? In order to generate scientific knowledge, appropriate procedure should be followed step by step. This is called a logical research sequence, which will be described in a six-step-model. The quality of research results is largely dependent on how these different steps have been followed. A so called "young science" has to be particularly conscious of this part of a meta-theory; in other words, it is important to develop good strategies for the research process in consideration of the specific characteristics of the field of movement, play and sport.

Section 4 deals with **"transfer of knowledge"** or with the question **"what is the practice-theory- and theory-practice-paradigm"**? The amount of available scientific evidence has become quite large in recent years. A lack in transferring knowledge to the practical application has become increasingly. Therefore, this fourth aspect of a meta-theory is of high actuality apparent for sport science. In this connection it is important to distinguish three different meanings of practice in regard to sport science, namely practice as sportaction, as professional practice in different sportspecific professional fields, and as the sum of the social reality of sport, which serves as target point for sport science research in a broad sense. Thus, these theory-practice (and vice versa) relationships have developed into a very fundamental issue of a scientific (meta theory), in this case of sport science.

At the end of this analysis **"concluding considerations"** are given. An attempt is made to summarize the main results, to give a critical evaluation, to indicate future directions for the scientific field called sport science, and to mention institutions and organizations which are important for the present status and future development of sport science.

Introductory Considerations

The topic of this analysis is a rather difficult one. Three aspects are combined in the main title of the research work and have to be viewed in light of their inter-relationship.

"Theoretical foundation" implies basic concepts, fundamental issues, and general justifications for sport science with the help of theoretical procedures. "Theory" or "theoretical" means that a solid reflection has taken place on these foundations, that they are well developed and assured in the light of scientific standards.

"Sport science" is the name for the "Wissenschaft", for the scientific work and its result related to a very complex social subsystem called sport. This phenomenon is very diversified, has many faces, and has to be seen in a multidimensional way. Thus, it is only logic, that the science, which deals with these issues, namely sport science, also shows a very complex character.

"Scientific discipline", indicates a branch within the wide field of the world of science. The historical development of science in general can be characterized as a constant process of differentiation and specification. Thus, many scientific disciplines exist today. Tomorrow, there will be even more, since the differentiation process has become a continuous one. In this context it has to be stated, that sport science is regarded as a very young discipline within the world of science, partly still attempting to get the full scientific recognition within the scientific community.

By relating these three aspects - "Theoretical Foundation"/"Sport Science"/"Scientific Discipline" - to each other a **"contribution to a philosophy (meta-theory) of sport science"** will be made. Thus, this subtitle of the given investigation and analysis stands for a program, an intention, and an endeavour to enhance the scientific character and acceptance of sport science ("Sportwissenschaft") in the world of science.

Purpose of this Investigation

In the interpretation of the title of this research report the **"Purpose of this Investigation"** is already mentioned. It is intended to reflect and analyse possible dimensions, by which sport science can be described and justified as a scientific discipline. This is done by dealing with theoretical foundations, which in turn are a contribution to a meta-theory of sport science.

Meta-theory or epistemology/scientific theory on a general level is a sub-discipline of philosophy as a scientific discipline. Meta-theory also has to be developed on the level of single scientific disciplines like sport science. In doing so it is important to take knowledge from general scientific theory, which is developed within the discipline of philosophy, into consideration.

At the same time the development of a **sport specific meta-theory** represents a contribution to the self understanding and perception of sport science. This is very important especially for a scientific field which is relatively young and still needs to receive recognition as a scientific discipline. Thus, the purpose of this investigation has - despite the theoretical approach - also a very pragmatic perspective, namely in regard to aspects of the scientific recognition of sport science within the scientific world.

Procedure for the Analysis

Based on the purpose of the investigation a certain **"Procedure for the Analysis"** had to be chosen. This procedure can be best described by using the so-called "Kieler Modell der Forschungsmethodologie" **(Kiel Model of Research Methodology)** (KMRM), which will be described in more detail in chapter 3. The model consists of the following 6 categories:

(1) The **"epistemology/scientific theory"** (philosophy), which leads to the undertaking of such an analysis is characterized by the following aspects: every scientific discipline must reflect its own history, status quo, and future development constantly in order to live up to world-wide accepted scientific standards.

(2) The **"research method"** of this investigation is characterized by description. Based on this description of the state of discussion regarding the meta-theory of sport science, theoretical concepts and models are developed; these may help to realise the purpose of this study, namely to develop theoretical foundations of sport science as a scientific discipline and thereby contribute to the formulation of a meta-theory of sport science.

(3) In consequence of this the **"research design"** is a survey design, comprising especially the discussion in the relevant German and English literature. This is at the same time an information for selecting the right sample of literature in order to gain data for this investigation.

(4) The relevant **"technique of data collection"** is therefore in this case content analysis, as it relates to the understanding of written facts. In most cases the data gained from this content analysis are coded in words.

(5) Therefore, the adequate **"technique of data analysis"** is the hermeneutical-oriented analysis of words, sentences and written texts. Due to the complexity of the given topic this is often a very difficult procedure, which must strive for the highest possible inter subjective evaluation in order to come up with objective, reliable and valid results. Even if it is not possible to attach numbers to these criteria in order to express the result of the research, it should be attempted to achieve high plausibility and objectivity .

(6) Finally, the aspect of **"knowledge transfer"** is considered in the procedure of this analysis by the fact, that the fourth area of the theoretical foundation of sport science, developed in this investigation, has the title: "Transfer of Knowledge in Sport Science. Or: What is the Practice - Theory and Theory - Practice Paradigm?"

The six described steps of the "KMRM" thus clearly indicate the procedure, which is used in this analysis, following a logic sequence in the realisation of certain steps within the process of gaining scientific knowledge.

Definition of Terms

In order to understand an investigation properly it is necessary to define certain terms as used in the study. The standards of scientific work are also related to the precision of the terminology used. The following terms are of high importance to this study:

"**Sport** is a specific form of human movement behaviour. Aims and objectives, the people participating in sport, time, and location are characterized by large diversity; this proves the central social relevance of the phenomenon, called sport. Sport is an expression of the cultural performance of man. Therefore, sport also has to do with the typical tendencies of bringing sport in close relation to ideology, profession, organisation, education, and science. Sport is part of a culture with an international character; socio-cultural diversity and special geographic conditions further increase the variability of sport. Sport is realised mainly in sport disciplines, which have varying importance according to the chosen context for action" (HAAG 1986a, 30-31).

Sport science represents a system of scientific research, teaching, and practice to which knowledge from other disciplines is integrated. It is the purpose and function of sport science to investigate questions, which have been identified as problems. Sport science is trying to gain knowledge in regard to the posed questions on a scientific basis. Finally, found solutions have to be applied, in order to explain, control, and if necessary change the practice of sport. Sport science is mainly visible through its body of knowledge, which is the result of the scientific endeavour in regard to sport. Sport science is a relatively young science. It is an example for a so-called theme-, integration-, interdisciplinary or cross disciplinary scientific field - in contrast to the long established sciences like philosophy, medicine, law, and mathematics which can be called discipline-oriented sciences.

Theory is understood as "any system of statements, which is characterized on one side through generality (form) and on the other side through the transcending of a mere stating of the here and now (content)" (KWIATKOWSKI 1985, 422). A scientific theory in turn is characterized by the fact, that its form is made explicit and its content is described with exact terms. Thus, theory is not an accidental result of science but also the aim and objective of science as well as an ideal, because in a theory knowledge can be structured in a clear, understandable and therefore informative manner.

Within scientific theory two kinds of theories are distinguished: empirical and deductive theories.

Empirical theories are built in an inductive way from statements on observations to proven hypotheses resulting in laws and finally to principles. The following figure expresses the sequence for the originating of empirical theories:

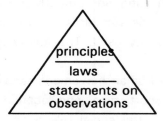

Fig. 1:   The Sequence for the Originating of Empirical Theories (HAAG)

In **deductive theories** statements are derived from axioms through logic processes. If the axioms are true, the derived theorems and assumptions are true as well, because they are proven. This deduction is made according to certain rules. Only by interpretation can such a formal system became true. The interpretation provides a field of application for the theory. Both are connected by rules for translation. The following figure illustrates the sequence for the originating of deductive theories:

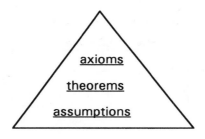

Fig. 2: The Sequence for the Originating of Deductive Theories (HAAG)

According to modern scientific theory the following points are considered to be characteristic for theories in a scientific sense.

— Theories can contain constructs (terms), which cannot be related directly to observable aspects. They can be observed only through their results and consequences (e.g. power, speed).
— It may be that two or more theories are in concurrence with each other. In that case it has to be decided based on experience which theory should be used in order to explain reality from a scientific point of view.
— The basic question is whether theories can be true. If the answer is yes, there could only be one theory in order to explain a specific aspect of reality.
— If theories are considered to be only more or less successful in predicting certain outcomes, then more than one acceptable theory can be available.
— The discussion within scientific theory today tends to state that it is not possible to have two comparable theories on the same issue (incommensurability).

Epistemology (known as "Erkenntnistheorie") is the summary term for theoretical considerations which relate to the modalities of gaining scientific knowledge, especially used in the philosophy of English speaking countries.

Scientific theory (known as "Wissenschaftstheorie") can also be characterized by a wide variety of terms like philosophy of science, meta-science, meta-theory, or logic of research. Basically, it stands for any kind of systematic form of dealing with science.
WILLIMCZIK (1987, 443-467) states that scientific theory itself or the philosophy of science can be seen as composed of different part-disciplines as indicated in the following figure:

	Scientific Theory or Philosophy of Science	
Ontology of Science		Metaphysics of Science
Real Sciences		Formal Sciences
Psychology)		Logic of Science
Sociology) of Science		
History)		

Fig. 3: Structure of Part Disciplines of a Scientific Theory
(WILLIMCZIK 1987, 443)

A philosophy (or ontology and metaphysics) of science, foundations of science, and scientific models are developed. The real and formal sciences then originate on the basis of this philosophy of science.

Four major questions, which also represent the main chapters of this scientific investigation, are characteristic for scientific theory (HAAG, STRAUß & HEINZE 1989):

(1) **Aims and objectives of sport science.** Or: What is the function of sport science?
(2) **The body of knowledge of sport science.** Or: What is the content of sport science?
(3) **Research methodology in sport science.** Or: What is the process of gaining scientific knowledge in sport science?
(4) **Transfer of knowledge in sport science.** Or: What is the practice - theory and theory - practice paradigm?

With these four questions a comprehensive view of the scientific theory in general and of the scientific theory in specific, as it relates to sport science, is given.

With the short explanation of these four terms - sport, sport science, theory, scientific theory - a basic frame of reference is given for this research study.

Thus, scientific theory , meta-theory, or a theory of the theory of sport science is the focus of this investigation.

Review of Literature

Before a conceptual model for a scientific - or meta-theory of sport science will be developed in chapter one to four a short **Review of Literature** on the scientific theory of sport science can give an insight into the discussion of this issue, which is very important for the development of a scientific field.

The discussion in German-speaking countries on the scientific theory of sport science can be summarised in the following way:

In 1939 ALTROCK wrote a paper entitled "Task and Extent of Sport Science". DIEM, who was a guiding figure for the development of German and international sport science, deals with questions of scientific theory related to physical exercises and sport as well ("Science of Physical Exercises", 1942; "Nature and Theory of Sport", 1949, 1960; "Sport Science as Pedagogy", 1953; "Sport as Science", 1957 - for literature compare WILLIMCZIK 1979, 174-190).

Since 1956 GROLL and FETZ have made intensive efforts to examine the question of the scientific character of physical exercises and physical education (GROLL 1956, 1957, 1959, 1961, 1973; FETZ 1961, 1964, 1966 - for literature compare WILLIMCZIK 1979, 174-190).

In the former German Democratic Republic (GDR) an intensive discussion of the way sport science sees itself was led after 1945 (WONNEBERGER 1954, 1965, 1968; TROGSCH 1962, 1973, 1975; ERBACH 1964, 1965, 1968, 1973, 1977; SIEGER 1965a,b,c; 1968 - for literature compare WILLIMCZIK 1979, 174-190).

A work published in 1987 (edited by BAUERSFELD) describes the newest state of the sport specific research methodological discussion in the former GDR ("Research Methods in Sport Methodic Scientific Disciplines"). The contribution by KUNATH (1988, 366-373) entitled "Differentiation and Integration in Sport Science" answers the question of the subject area of sport science from the former GDR point of view. An article by BERNETT (1980, 375-403), which analyses the "Development and Structure of Sport Science in the Former GDR", should be recognised here as well.

In the Federal Republic of Germany SCHMITZ addressed the discussion of "The Problem of a 'Science' of Physical Exercises and Sport" in 1966. GRUPE has had an influence on the discussion of scientific theory until the present day (1968, 1971, 1973, 1977, 1986). He has emphasised that the development of this "young" scientific discipline should occur with a sense of proportion and on a solid basis. His initiatives to publish the journal "Sportwissenschaft" (Sport Science, since 1971) has made an essential contribution towards the establishment of sport science as a scientific discipline.

WILLIMCZIK has also influenced the development of the discussion of scientific theory; proceeding from his work entitled "Scientific Theory Aspects of Sport Science" (1968) he has expressed his views in several contributions on problems of scientific theory (e.g. WILLIMCZIK 1980, 337-359, 1985, 9-32). In 1979 he published a reader volume of "Scientific Theory Contributions to Sport Science". His introductory article "Scientific Theory Problems of Sport Science - Attempts of a Comparative Analysis" (1979, 11-56) (shortened and edited version in the "Handbook Sport Science" by EBERSPÄCHER 1987, 443-467) contains a synoptic-comparative presentation of the development of the scientific theoretical foundation of sport science. Contributions in this volume give insight to the state of discussion in the United States, Canada and the Federal Republic of Germany. With the production of three volumes on problems of "Research Methods in Sport Science" (Vol.1 Statistics, Vol.2/3 Basic Course in Data Collection). WILLIMCZIK has advanced the research methodological discussions as part of a scientific theory with respect to sport science (1975, 1983; with SINGER 1985).

Since the late seventies HAAG (1979), has strived for the creation of a concept of the subject area of sport science with the development of the Seven-Theory-Field-Model (sports medicine, sport biomechanics, sport psychology, sport pedagogy, sport sociology, sport history, sport philosophy). He has lead the research methodological discussion mainly from the approach of comparative sport science research (HAAG n.y., 28-40) and from the viewpoint of sport pedagogy (HAAG 1983, 53-81) (development of a logical research sequence model: foundations with respect to scientific theory; research methods; research designs, data collection techniques; data analysis techniques; aspects of knowledge transfer). These research methodological themes are and will be analysed in detail in the five volume work entitled "Foundations for the Study of Sport Science" (compare volumes I-V, HAAG & STRAUß 1989, 1990, 1991, 1994).

Substantial contributions towards the discussion of the self- understanding of sport science originate from the scientific advisory board of the DSB (German Sport Federation) (compare HEINEMANN & BECKER 1986). HEINEMANN has also strongly promoted the scientific theory discussion related to sport science as the director of this advisory board of the DSB (compare HEINEMANN 1980, 360-374; 1985, 33-45).

The discussion regarding the development of sport science has always been a main issue. Proceeding from occasionally detectable uncertainty with respect to the position of sport science in the context of sciences. RITTNER (1974, 357-371) attempts to justify the body and its fate in society as the subject of sport science. MEINBERG (1981a, 406-419; 1981b) suggests to reach systematics of sport science through system theoretical considerations. LIEBER (1988, 125-136) pleads for pluralism of subjects (sport sciences) and pluralism of methods.

The research methodological discussion is an essential aspect of scientific theory considerations next to the question of the research subject or body of knowledge. WILLIMCZIK (1975, 1983); SINGER & WILLIMCZIK (1985) and HAAG & STRAUß (1989, 1990, 1991, 1994) have provided sources for this discussion.

The discussion is led with respect to individual theory fields. Examples are: Sport Biomechanics (BALLREICH & KUHLOW 1980a,b), Sport Psychology (BÖS & ROTH 1978), Sport Pedagogy (MEINBERG 1979a; 1979b; HAAG 1983; GRUPE 1984b), Sport Sociology (LENK & LÜSCHEN 1976; BECKER 1983; ERDMANN 1988), Sport History (BERNETT 1984) and Sport Philosophy (HAAG 1989c).

The scientific theory of sport science as an aspect of sport philosophy should not so much balance deficits and uncertainities regarding the scientific self-understanding of sport science; but should rather make constructive meta-theoretical discussion possible, which is necessary for a young scientific field such as sport science. Sport science is also impending on new challenges from post-industrial society (WATSON 1986, 245-267). According to BAUR (1988, 361-386) new development-theoretical conceptions (interaction, transactional and dialectic aspects) are crucial for the further development of sport science.

The four-step strategy of the introductory considerations (purpose - procedure - definition of terms and review of literature) can thus provide a framework for the development of theoretical foundations of sport science as a scientific discipline in the following four chapters, intending to make a contribution to the development of a scientific theory or a meta-theory of sport science.

1. Aims and Objectives of Sport Science. Or: What is the Function of Sport Science?

Introduction

To pose the "final" question: "What for?", "Why?", "What is the Intention?" etc. is a fundamental problem in human life. It is important from an anthropological point of view to ask these questions, because the acting of human beings has to have some sense, direction and justification. Throughout history people have asked themselves: Why we as human beings are so curious? Why are do we always want to know more and generate an increasing amount of scientific information and knowledge?

If a phenomenon such as sport is gaining more and more social acceptance and importance, the existence of scientific endeavour to continuously generate knowledge is obvious. Thus, it is legitimate to pose this fundamental question for the perception of a scientific field, namely: **"What is the Function of Sport Science?"**

Four dimensions are analysed in which an answer to this question can be given. All four dimensions will generate and produce different points of view, producing a wide range of aspects composing a comprehensive answer.

Although sport science is a young and newly existing scientific field, the **history of sport science** or the science of physical activity can be traced back to the beginning of this century, not considering the many interpretations which were given by leading philosophers and medical scholars before 1900. Historical considerations provide a wider framework in searching for an answer to the question or can contribute to understanding the present-day perception of sport science in a better way.

A horizontal perspective is implied in the **comparative dimension**; it relates to a comparison of the question at hand and given answers in at least two different socio-cultural settings or countries. By collecting information for answering a question from the point of view of different countries the variety of aspects, ideas and solutions can increase tremendously. The advantage of using the comparative approach is threefold:

— More information about other countries and their systems is gained.
— A better insight into one's own system is achieved.
— Ideas for improvement of the own situation or point of view can result.

Therefore, comparative studies may help to reach well justified and solid answers to the given question: "What is the function of sport science?" These answers then will not be limited to a one-sided view from one country. Since movement, play, and sport are typical international phenomena, it seems very useful and necessary to follow this broader international, comparative perspective.

The **status-quo or present-day dimension** mean, that the situation today is analysed very carefully in regard to finding answers to the question. It will predominantly consist of an analysis of relevant present literature in sport science published within the last decade. Even if the process of the development of sport science to a fully established and recognised academic discipline is not yet at a satisfactory stage, statements of opinion are available in regard to the stated question. A young and developing scientific field has to constantly discuss and reconsider its own meta-theory in order to reach a sound development of the scientific field. Therefore, this present-day dimension in regard to the question "What is the function of sport science?" is of considerable importance.

Last but not least, some reflections on a **futuristic dimension** may help to define the aims and objectives of sport science. This dimension is more of a hypothetical nature and not scientifically proven. However, it is the task of the field of higher education and scholars involved in university work to think ahead, to develop perspectives and to work on concepts for the future, based on a sound historical knowledge and a well balanced present-day understanding.

These four dimensions, unfold thoughts and ideas, which may be helpful in order to come up with useful answers to the question: "What is the function of sport science?" In this manner a contribution to the meta-theory of sport science may result which can promote the further development of the academic field of sport science.

1.1. Historical Dimension

In this context "historical dimension" cannot mean a lengthy analysis of texts, documents and literature which deals with "aims and objectives of sport science: Or: What is the function of sport science?" In "review of literature", within the introductory considerations, a short overview of the discussion of scientific theory (meta-theory) in German sport science literature has been provided. This short review also gives some ideas related to certain positions within the scientific theory of sport science from a historical perspective.

In the following short analysis it is attempted to include parts of documents, which indicate the development of sport, sport education and sport science on the national (German) and international level. By using these selected texts it may be seen that the objectives and function of sport science is not new and that one can learn from earlier point of views in relation to present situations and possibly influence the future development of sport science. Examples on the national and international level are from a 30 year period (between 1955 and 1985):

In **1955** the "**Kuratorium für die sportmedizinische Forschung**" (Council for Research in Sports Medicine) passed statutes (HAAG, KIRSCH & KINDERMANN 1991, 167): "The council for sport medicine research, founded by the German Sport Federation, has the task to do research in sport medicine in order to serve the people, especially the youth. It should deal with all important questions from this field, summarise research, co-ordinate, and guide future research".

In **1964** the "**Zentralkomitee für die Forschung auf dem Gebiet des Sports**" (Central Committee for Research in Sport) was founded and passed statutes. In § 2 is listed (HAAG, KIRSCH & KINDERMANN 1991, 171-172): " ... scientific purposes ... by: Attesting and supporting sport science research and the dealing with related questions by: (1) Finding unsolved problems for sport science research, which have fundamental importance for physical education; (2) incentives and co-ordination for all research projects and control on the realisation of the tasks put forward by the committee under scientific criteria; (3) to give research grants in the different theory fields to well known and experienced researchers for scientific work, which is especially needed to benefit the people; ... (4) dissemination of the newest research results from sport science research".

In **1966** the "**Charta des deutschen Sports**" (The Charter of German Sport) was accepted as the basic document for sport in the Federal Republic of Germany. From five major points one is devoted to sport and science (HAAG, KIRSCH & KINDERMANN 1991, 11): "Sport and physical education give the sciences several tasks; institutions of higher learning are also deciding today on their development and status in our society. Only with the help of the institutions of higher learning will it be possible to overcome the biased ideas on education. In order to reach this aim it is necessary to: secure research and teaching in regard to sport and physical education by installing professorships (chairs) for sport science; enlarge the institutes for physical education within the institutions of higher education; secure an equal position for physical education as a subject for study and examination in comparison to other school-subjects regarding regulations for study and examination of future physical education teachers".

In **1976** the **"Deutsche Vereinigung für Sportwissenschaft"** (DVS) was founded. § 2, 1 of the statutes includes (HAAG, KIRSCH & KINDERMANN 1991, 179): "The DVS is following the aim to promote the further development of sport science. Its tasks are especially: Generating and supporting sport science research; initiating and organising scientific communication between and within the theory fields of sport science; determining questions of study and teaching in sport science; supporting the development of the structure of sport science institutes; promoting young sport scientists; furthering the development of a science - like and actual structure for the personnel in sport science institutes; representing the interests of sport science in national and international organisations and institutions".

In **1978** the **"International Charter for Physical Education and Sport"** was adopted by UNESCO. Article 6 deals with sport science (HAAG, KIRSCH & KINDERMANN 1991, 54): "Research and evaluation are necessary parts of the development of physical education and sport. 6.1 Research and evaluation in physical education and sport should promote the advancement of all forms of sport and contribute to improve health and the security of people engaging in sport as well as the training methods and the methods for organisation and administration. The educational system will profit from new plans, which intend to provide better teaching methods and a higher standard of performance. 6.2 Scientific research - the social consequence of this should not be overlooked - has to prevent prohibited applications of physical education and sport".

In **1983 "The International Council of Sport Science and Physical Education"** (ICSSPE) adopted statutes containing interesting statements on sport science (HAAG, KIRSCH & KINDERMANN 1991, 186-187):
"Art. 1: ICSSPE is an international organisation concerned with the promotion and dissemination of results and findings in the field of sport science and their practical application in cultural and educational contexts. ...
Art. 3: The fundamental objectives of ICSSPE / CIEPSS shall be: to encourage international co-operation in the field of sport science for the benefit of all; to promote, stimulate and co-ordinate scientific research in the field of physical education and sport throughout the world and to support the application of its results in vari-

ous practical areas of sport; to make scientific knowledge of sport and practical experiences available to all national and international organisations and institutions of sport science, especially those in developing countries; ... to facilitate differentiation in sport science whilst promoting the integration of the various branches.

Art. 4: To achieve these objectives ICSSPE / CIEPSS shall: encourage and promote the co-ordination of activities in sport science on an international scale as well as the collection, analysis and dissemination of knowledge in the field of sport science and sport practice; initiate, co-ordinate and organise international conferences, symposia, meetings, seminars, and clinics; ... stimulate and provide for the publication of knowledge in sport science and encourage the mass media to spread the idea and results; co-operate with national and other international organisations in the field of physical education and sport, sport science, and other sciences".

In this important ICSSPE document six examples from a time period of 30 years (1955-1985) are given in order to illustrate, which ideas and concepts regarding the aims, objectives, and functions of sport science have been expressed nationally and internationally. Examples for documents appearing after 1985 are included in part 1.3 "status-quo or present-day dimension", since they still seem to have strong influence at present.

There are, of course, other parameters by which the "historical dimension" can be analysed. One very interesting example in this context is the development of the Olympic Scientific Congresses from 1909 in Paris (France) until 1992 in Malaga (Spain). This is presented in an analysis by KIRSCH (1990, 325-340). The analysis of the programs and course offerings of the Departments of Physical Education or Sport Science Institutes could be another approach. Internationally this would have to be done by consulting AIESEP and analysing their material. For Germany (at least the "old" FRG) the book series "Das Studium der Leibeserziehung - heute Sportwissenschaft" ("The Study of Physical Education - today Sport Science") (DSLV 1967-1994) represents an interesting reference work.

BERNETT (1980) has given an extensive historical analysis of the **former GDR system** relating to sport science.

Even if the relaying of historical insights was and is not always preferred, the given examples show how rich the information is which can be found in the historical dimension. A future direction of sport science research should be to devote time to the historical dimension before "hurrying" to a new project. Often there are very valuable insights available in a historical context. Ideas and concepts are not always brand new. A little reference to the historical dimension could also be helpful for avoiding parallel research efforts on the same issue (GRUPE 1968, 1971).

1.2. Comparative Dimension

In the "Introductory Considerations" an explanation was provided for why a comparative dimension might generate further insights into the issue of aims, objectives, and functions of sport science. Since comparison as a research paradigm (HAAG 1982B) can be used under different socio-cultural points of view - as long as at least two different socio-cultural settings are involved - it seems feasible to present a figure in which **comparison as a research paradigm** is explained; thus it can be applied to the topic of aims, objectives, and functions of sport science (BENNETT, HOWELL & SIMRI 1983; HAAG 1982b).

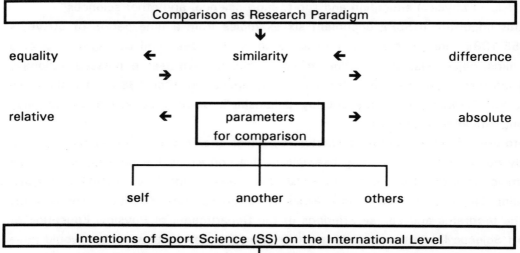

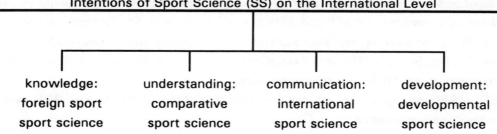

Fig. 4:   An Intercultural-Comparative Research Strategy (HAAG 1990, 309)

It is indicated in this figure that many aspects have to be considered in a comparative research paradigm. It is especially important to understand that research on the international level is more than comparative. The knowledge pattern (foreign sport science) precedes the understanding pattern (comparative sport science). The communication and development pattern may follow as a special task. Within this short outline of the comparative dimension, the discussion on aims, objectives, and functions of sport science in the **USA** is taken as an **example**; this is due to the fact, that the author of this analysis is developing the concepts from a German point of view. Eventually models from other countries could be offered for comparative purposes. The presentation of aspects regarding USA falls within the so - called foreign sport science. The comparison dimension in regard to the topic of aims, objectives, and functions of sport science can then be understood (HAAG 1990, 308-324).

The **aims, objectives and functions of sport science** in the **USA** are discussed predominantly in the journal **Quest** (published by NAPEHE) and in the "**The Academy Papers**" (published by the American Academy of kinesiology and Physical Education).

HENRY (1970, 282), a major authority in physical education in the USA, wrote: "If the academic discipline of physical education did not already exist, it would need to be invented". For a long time the discussion was always dealing with the question: Is there something like an academic discipline of physical education? ABERNATHY and WALTZ (1964) see the central function of physical education as an academic discipline in the study of human movement under the categories of physical limits, movement experiences, personality structure, personal perception, social-cultural environment. KLEINMAN (1968) gave a warning, that the theory-building should not be too limited, so that the structure of movement, play, and sport is not seen too narrow and too fixed. He advocates an open discussion of the function of sport science and therefore even requires a so-called "non-theory of sport". GREENDORFER (1987) points to the trend towards specialisation and fragmentation in sport science, which makes integrated concepts impossible. ROSE (1986, 1-21) supports this point of view by seeing a future direction for sport science in a cross-disciplinary, research-oriented conception and in using "movement as means of expression" as the central core of sport science.

Other sources for topics of a scientific theory like "aims, objectives, and function of sport science" are periodical conferences, where the position and function of sport science within the study at institutions of Higher Education are discussed (NAPEHE 1976; LAWSON 1988). Just recently, two "Academy Papers" have been published, along this line; they deal with sport science or kinesiology, the name proposed by the "American Academy of Kinesiology and Physical Education" in a resolution made in April 19, 1989) and with the relation to professional training. Nr. 23 (AAPE, 1990) "The Evolving Undergraduate Major" and Nr. 24 (AAPE 1991) "New Possibilities, New Paradigms?" deal with graduate education and have made contributions to questions of sport science (kinesiology) in regard to the core in professional training at the undergraduate and graduate level. The naming of institutions of higher learning also indicates an open situation as to what term should be used (e.g. kinesiology, sport science, sport studies, exercise science, physical activity science, physical education or kinanthropology).

In summary, a clear trend can be observed in USA science in general, but also in sport science/kinesiology in specific: Stopping fragmentation, overspecialisation, dealing predominantly with very small issues, one-sided research approaches etc. It is clear that it is also the function of sport science/kinesiology to reform research approaches in order to be able to investigate the world like it is, in its variety, its ecological validity, its overt and hidden dimensions. Sport science/kinesiology should apply more integrative and interdisciplinary thinking, thus being able to get closer to reality within the research process. In general the aims, objectives, and functions of sport science are seen to a greater extent under criteria like flexibility, proximity to reality, holistic and not too specific approaches, social relevance, long term effects, social responsibility, and contributions to promote humanity.

These short aspects of the scientific discussion in the USA may encourage one to bring these points in juxtaposition with ideas in a specific country in regard to the given topic of aims, objectives, and functions of sport science and thus applying the comparative approach.

It is clear, that a comparative approach could be applied also to the three other major issues of a scientific- or meta-theory of sport science (body of knowledge / research methodology / transfer of theory to practice).

The comparative dimension, however, is presented in this analysis only to explain its paradigmatic character. The "aims, objectives, and functions of sport science" topic was chosen to describe the four models (historic, comparative, status-quo, futuristic) with their specific access and also in their common features.

Further information on the **comparative research paradigm** can be found in material, published by the **"International Society for Comparative Physical Education and Sport"** (ISCPES). Such as the **"Journal of Comparative Physical Education and Sport: Cross-cultural and International studies"** and congress reports (SIMRI 1979; POOLEY & POOLEY 1982; KROTEE & JAEGER 1986; HAAG, BENNETT & KAYSER 1986; BROOM, CLUMPNER, PENDLETON & POOLEY 1988; Fu & SPEAKS 1989; STANDEVEN, HARDMAN & FISHER 1991).

1.3. Status-quo or Present-day Dimension

Status-quo or present-day does not mean taking only one picture. It more or less relates to the present time, characterized by the development in the recent years. There are several parameters with which the present status of aims, objectives, and functions of sport science can be analysed. This is done in a dual approach, i.e. examples are taken from Germany and from the international level for every parameter. The following three parameters will be used:

(1) **Terminology of the scientific discipline,**

(2) **sport science organisations including respective scientific journals, and**

(3) **key documents under a comparative perspective.**

(1) The **terminology** relates to the name of the scientific discipline as derived from the name of the institutions of higher learning or as proposed by relevant professional societies.

(1a) Germany: Names of the institutions of higher learning related to sport

In Germany exist at present 68 institutions of higher learning related to sport. They all have the status of a scientific institution, including the right to grant a Ph.D. or Ed.D. Some are still exempt from granting the degree acquired by a so-called "habilitation".

This is a degree which is normally necessary in order to become a professor with tenure. After 1945-50 the development of these sport science institutes has been quite steady. First they were named "institutes for physical activity" or "institutes for physical education". Starting with the 1970's the term physical education was more and more replaced by the word sport, meaning in German all kind of physical activities, not only top level athletics like in the English language.

In connection with the Olympic Games 1972 in Munich the founding of sport science institutes increased very fast and thus the variety became larger; this had again consequences in regard to the names of these institutes: examples are listed in the following table:

Name of the Institution	Number	Name of the Institution	Number
Institut für Sportwissen-schaft(en)	24	Fachbereich Sport	1
Fachbereich Sportwissen-schaft	5	Fachrichtung Sportwissen-schaft	1
Institut für Sport und Sport-wissenschaft	4	Fach Leibeserziehung	1
Sportzentrum	3	Deutsche Sporthochschule	1
Fach Sport	3	Fakultät Sportwissenschaft (in Gründung)	1
Fakultät für Sportwissenschaft	2	Institut für Spiel und Bewe-gungserziehung	1
Institut für Sport und seine Di-daktik	2	Institut für Sport	1
Fach Sport und Sportpädago-gik	2	Institut für Sportwissenschaft und Motologie	1
Institut für Sportwissenschaft und Sport	1	Zentralinstitut für Sportwis-senschaft	1
Sportinstitut	1	Fachgebiet Sport und Sport-wissenschaften	1
Fachbereich Sportpädagogik	1	Sportwissenschaftliches Institut	1
Institut für Ästhetische Erzie-hung und Sportdidaktik	1	Staatliche Sportlehrerausbil-dung	1
Lehrgebiet Sport und Sport-pädagogik	1	Institut für Sportwissen-schaft/Sportzentrum	1
Betriebseinheit Sportwissen-schaft und allgemeiner Hoch-schulsport	1	Sektion Sportwisschenschaft	1
Institut für Sportwissen-schaft/Sportpädagogik	1		

Tab. 1: Overview on Names of Institutions of Higher Learning Related to Sport in Germany (HAAG)

It is quite obvious that the tendency goes towards the usage of the term sport science, which is a clear indication that sport stands for a comprehensive system and not just athletics.

(1b) International: Resolution of the American Academy of Kinesiology and Physical Education 1989)

The "American Academy of Kinesiology and Physical Education" (AAKPE) is the leading organisation for sport science in the USA. It is a group consisting of the most prominent sport scientists. The opinions, statements, and resolutions of AAKPE provide some guideline for the development in the USA, but to a certain extent - due to the fact that the English language is the language of science accepted world-wide - also in other parts of the world.

Resolution of AAKPE (AAPE 1990, 104)

Whereas the number and diversity of descriptors of academic programs and administrative units related to the study of human movement is now in excess of 100, and;

Whereas the basic conceptual framework of this body of knowledge differs from university campus to campus, and;

Whereas a multitude of degree titles, program names, and administrative rubrics has produced confusion regarding the nature of the study of movement, even among academicians who work in the field, and;

Whereas unanimity in description and a nationally accepted definition of the body of knowledge would provide a stronger sense of purpose, higher visibility in the academic community, and a greater understanding of the discipline by the public;

Therefore, be it resolved that the Academy recommends that the subject matter core content for undergraduate baccalaureate degrees related to the study of movement be called kinesiology, and that baccalaureate degrees in the academic discipline be titled kinesiology.

The Academy encourages administrative units, such as departments or divisions, in which the academic study of kinesiology is predominant, to adopt the name kinesiology. Finally, in any situation in which an administrative unit feels comfortable in describing the totality of its components by the title of the body of knowledge, the Academy recommends that this descriptor be kinesiology.

Comment

The purpose of the resolution is to give description to an academic discipline. The resolution is not intended to legislate changes in professional preparation programs and/or degrees. Kinesiology is the study of human motion. Among key concepts in this body of knowledge are (1) energy, work, and efficiency, (2) co-ordination, control, and skill, (3) growth, development, and form, (4) culture, values, and achievement.

After having been established for a long time, the term physical education as a name for the academic discipline - despite the fact, that physical education is a process and not a proper name for an academic discipline dealing with the very complex phenomena of movement, play, and sport - today the majority in North America seems to accept the term kinesiology. This term, however, is more oriented towards the medical-natural science base of the field. Unfortunately the word sport does not have the broad meaning in English as in many other languages, and therefore it is obviously difficult to accept the term sport science, where sport always means the total subsystem of a given society (HAAG 1970).

(2)   In regard to **sport science organisations** and the respective **sport science journals** a category system is needed for presenting an overview. Since such a system, is used (see chapter 2) it also functions as a basis for this short overview on sport science organisations and sport science journals. On the one hand, the statutes of these sport science-related organisations and the concepts of the respective sport science journals are a representative indicator of the status-quo or present-day dimension of the topic at hand. On the other hand they give many detailed answers to questions regarding aims, objectives, and functions of sport science.

The national (Germany), and international dimension is combined in the following table, thus allowing for an overall evaluation of the provided data. The material for Germany is not translated, since the major purpose of listing material for Germany is to give the international audience an insight into a national situation. Of major interest is for shure the international dimension.

The four tables relate to **"established theory fields"**, **"new theory fields"**, **"theme fields - sport specific"**, and **"theme fields - general"**.

The categories of the tables are always organisation and journal for both the national and international level.

Theory Field (longer existing)	Organisation (Germany)	Journal (Germany)	Organisation (international)	Journal (international)
1. Sportmedizin (Sport Medicine)	Deutscher Sportärztebund (DSÄB); Gesellschaft für orthopädisch-traumatologische Sportmedizin (GOTS)	Deutsche Zeitschrift für Sportmedizin; Österreichisches Journal für Sportmedizin; Schweizer Zeitschrift für Sportmedizin; Sportverletzungen, Sportschäden	Federation International de Medicine Sportive (FIMS); International Association of Olympic Medical Officers (IAOMO); Biochemistry of Exercise (ICSSPE-Committee); International Working Group on Ergonometry (IWGE)(ICSSPE-Committee); Confederation Europeene pour la Therapie Physique (CETP)	American Journal of Sports Medicine; Australian Journal of Sports Medicine; British Journal of Sports Medicine; Canadian Journal of Applied Physiology; International Journal of Sport Medicine; International Journal of Sport Nutrition; Medicine and Science in Sports and Exercise; Pediatric Exercise Science; Physical Fitness Sports Medicine; The Journal of Sport Medicine and Physical Fitness
2. Sportbiomechanik (Sport Biomechanics)	Sektion "Biomechanik" der dvs		International Society for the Advancement of Kinanthropometry (ISAK); World Commission of Sport Biomechanics	International Journal of Sport Biomechanics (IJSB); Journal of Applied Biomechanics
3. Sportpsychologie (Sport Psychology)	Arbeitsgemeinschaft für Sportpsychologie (ASP) (als Sektion der DVS); Sportpsychologie für die Praxis	psychologie und sport	Federation Europeenne de Psychologie des Sports et des Activites Corporelle (FEPSAC); International Society of Sport Psychology (ISSP)	International Journal of Sport Psychology; Journal of Sport and Exercise Psychology (JSEP); The Sport Psychologist (TSP)
4. Sportpädagogik (Sport Pedagogy)	Forschungsgruppe Unterrichtsmedien im Sport e.V. (FUS); Kommission "Sportpädagogik" der Deutschen Gesellschaft für Erziehungswissenschaft; Sektion "Sportpädagogik" der DVS	Sportpädagogik; Sportunterricht; Körpererziehung; Sport Praxis	International Association for Physical Education in Higher Education (AIESEP); International Committee of Sport Pedagogy (ICSP); International Society for Comparative Physical Education and Sport (ISCPES); Internationaler Arbeitskreis für Zeitgemäße Leibeserziehung (IAZL)	International Journal of Physical Education; Journal of Comparative Physical Education and Sport (Cross-cultural and International Studies); Journal of Teaching in Physical Education (JTPE)
5. Sportsoziologie (Sport Sociology)	Sektion "Sportsoziologie" der DVS	Olympische Jugend	International Committee for Sociology of Sport (ICSS); North American Society for the Sociology of Sport (NASSS); "Sport and Developing Countries"-Working Group (ICSSPE)	International Review for the Sociology of Sport; Journal of Sport & Social Issues; Journal of Sport Management (ISM); Sociology of Sport Journal; Sport Sociology Bulletin
6. Sportgeschichte (Sport History)	Sektion "Sportgeschichte" der DVS; Carl-Diem-Institut; Deutsches Sportmuseum; Niedersächsisches Institut für Sportgeschichte Hoya e.V.	Nikephoros; Sozial- und Zeitgeschichte des Sports; Olympisches Feuer	International Society for the History of Physical Education and Sport (ISHPES); International Olympic Academy (IOA)	Arena; Journal of Sport History; Stadion; The British Journal of Sport History
7. Sportphilosophie (Sport Philosophy)	Sektion "Sportphilosophie" der DVS		Philosophic Society for the Study of Sport (PSSS); Nature and Function of Sport Science (ICSSPE-Committee)	Journal of the Philosophy of Sport

Tab. 2.1: Organisations and Journals Related to Sport Science (Established Theory Fields) (HAAG & HEIN 1990, 401-402)

Theory Field (new)	Organisation (Germany)	Journal (Germany)	Organisation (international)	Journal (international)
1. Sportinformation (Sport Information)	Arbeitsgemeinschaft der Sportwissenschaftlichen Bibliotheken (AGSP) Fachbereich "Fachinformation" (BISp)		International Association for Sports Information (IASI)	International Bulletin of Sports Information
2. Sportpolitik (Sport Politics)		Hochschulsport Olympisches Feuer Olympische Jugend Sozial- und Zeitgeschichte des Sports	Sport and Developing Countries (ICSSPE-Committee)	International Review for the Sociology of Sport
3. Sportrecht (Sport Law)	Aufgabenbereich "Rechts- Sozial- und Steuerfragen" (DSB) ISS der Universität Bayreuth Willi-Weyer-Akademie Berlin (FVA)		International Association of Sport Law (I.A.S.L.)	Journal of Sport Management (JSM)
4. Übungsstätten/Geräte (Facilities/Equipment)	Fachbereich "Sportstätten und Sportgeräte" (BISp)		International Working Group for the Construction of Sport- and Leisure Facilities (IAKS) World Federation of the Sporting Goods Industry	Sportstättenbau- und Bäderanlagen
5. Sportökonomie (Sport Economy)	ISS der Universität Bayreuth Institut für Soziologie der Universität Hamburg	Sportreport: Aktuelle Ergebnisse der sportwissenschaftlichen Forschung (Sportwissenschaft und Sportartikelwirtschaft)	International Society of Sports Sponsors (ISSS) North American Society for Sports Management (NASSM)	Journal of Sport Management (JSM) Sport Sponsor (Newsletter)

Tab 2.2: Organisations and Journals Related to Sport Science (New Theory Fields) (HAAG & HEIN 1990, 414-415)

Theme Field (Sport Specific)	Organisation (Germany)	Journal (Germany)	Organisation (international)	Journal (international)
1. Movement Science - Movement Theory - "Bewegungslehre"	Aktionskreis für Psychomotorik e. V. Sektion "Sportmotorik" der dvs	Motorik (Zeitschrift für Motopädagogik und Mototherapie)	International Society for "Sportmotorik"	Journal of Human Movement Studies Journal of Motor Behavior Movement Perceptual and Motor Skills
2. Play Science - Play Theory - "Spiellehre"	Sektion "Sportphilosophie" und "Sportpädagogik" der dvs		International Playground Association (IPA) The Association for the Study of Play (TASP)	Play & Culture
3. Training Science - Training Theory - "Trainingslehre"	Sektion "Trainingswissenschaft" der dvs Trainerakademie Köln Verband Deutscher Diplomtrainer (VDDT)	Leistungssport Informationen der Trainerakademie des DSB, Köln		American Coach Athletic Coach Athletic Journal Scholastic Coach
4. Instruction Science - Instruction Theory - "Unterrichtslehre" (Didaktik) (of Sport)	Sektion "Sportpädagogik" der dvs Forschungsgruppe Unterrichtsmedien im Sport e. V. (FUS) Kommission "Sportpädagogik der DGfJ	Sportunterricht (v.a. Lehrhilfen) Körpererziehung Sport Praxis Sportpädagogik	Internationaler Arbeitskreis für zeitgemäße Leibeserziehung (IAZL) International Committee of Sport Pedagogy (ICSP) International Association of Physical Education and Sport for Girls and Women (IAPESGW) International Council for Health, Physical Education, and Recreation (ICHPER) International Federation of Physical Education (FIEP)	Teaching Elementary Physical Education Journal of Physical Education, Recreation, and Dance (AAHPERD)

Tab. 2.3: Organisations and Journals Related to Sport Science (Theme Fields - Sport Specific) (HAAG & HEIN 1990, 420)

Theme Field (General)	Organisation (Germany)	Journal (Germany)	Organisation (international)	Journal (international)
1. Performance and Performance Ability in Sport	Bundesausschuß für Leistungssport (BAL)	Leistungssport	International Committee on Physical Fitness Research (ICPFR)	Journal of Strength and Conditioning Research
2. Music and Movement	Deutscher Gymnastikbund Verband Deutscher Sport- und Gymnastikschulen (VDSG)	Rhythmus Ballett-Journal Das Tanzarchiv		Impulse (The International Journal of Dance Science, Medicine, and Education)
3. Sport and Recreation	Bundesausschuß für Breitensport (DSB) Deutsche Gesellschaft für Freizeit e.V. Sport mit Einsicht e.V.	Animation und Freizeit	Sport and Leisure (ICSSPE-Committee) World Leisure and Recreation Association (WLRA)	Journal of Leisure Research Journal of Physical Education, Recreation, and Dance (AAHPERD) Leisure Studies WLRA-Journal
4. Sport and Health	Bundesvereinigung für Gesundheitserziehung Deutscher Verband für Gesundheitssport und Sporttherapie e. V. (DVGS) Forschungsgemeinschaft zur Gesundheitsförderung durch Bewegungspädagogik e. V. (FGB e.V.) Forschungs- und Beratungsstelle für Gesundheit, Sport und Ernährung (GeSpuEr-Bremen)	Herz, Sport & Gesundheit Sporttherapie in Theorie und Praxis	World Health Organization (WHO)	Health Education (AAHPERD)
5. Sport with Special Groups	Aktionskreis für Psycho-Motorik e.V. Arbeitsstelle "Behindertensport" in Berlin Bundesarbeitsgemeinschaft zur Förderung haltungsgefährdeter Kinder und Jugendlicher Deutscher Behindertensportverband	Haltung und Bewegung Motorik Krankengymnastik	International Federation of Adapted Physical Activity (IFAPA) European Association for Research Into Adapted Physical Activity (EARAPA) North American Federation for Adapted Physical Activity (NAFAPA) Asian Society for Adapted Physical Education and Exercise (ASAPE)	The Adapted Physical Activity Quarterly (APAQ) Journal of Aging and Physical Activity Journal of Sport Rehabilitation
6. Sport and Mass Media	Arbeitsgruppe "Sport und Literatur" der dvs Verband deutscher Sportjournalisten (VDS)	Medien und Sport	Association Internationale de la Presse Sportive (AIPS) Sport and Mass Media (ICSSPE-Committee) Union Europeene de la Presse Sportive (UEPS)	Journal of Sport Literature
7. Aggression and Violence in Sport	"Fair geht vor" (DOG, DSB, NOK)		Entente pour un Sport sans violence et pour le Fair Play (ESSVFP) International Committee for Fair Play (ICFP) International Foundation Rika de Backer-van Ocker for the fight against Violence associated with Sport	

Tab. 2.4: Organisations and Journals Related to Sport Science (Theme Fields -General)(HAAG & HEIN 1990, 423)

(3) In regard to the **documents** two key examples are chosen which represent aspects of the current development.

(3a) Germany: Resolution for the continued development of sport science (1985) (HAAG, KIRSCH & KINDERMANN 1991, 190-191)

Since its beginnings in 1950 the German Sport Federation (DSB) has supported the development of sport science to a great extent. From time to time resolutions and statements have been adapted by the DSB and thus brought to public attention. As a result of a crisis regarding sport science in 1985 the following resolution was adopted by the DSB in order to promote the function of sport science in the future:

"Sport science has developed during the last twenty years in to a scientific discipline recognised widely by universities, ministries of culture, and sport organisations. The German Sport Federation (DSB) has strongly promoted and supported this development. The DSB has:

— demanded the instalment of chairs for sport sience 1950,
— co-operated in the founding of the "Federal Institute of Sport Science",
— supported young scientists by creating the Carl Diem-Science-Competition and the Herman Altrock-Scholarship,
— initiated and supported the journal "Sportwissenschaft",
— supported the "Deutsche Vereinigung für Sportwissenschaft" (DVS) to a great extent in its work towards recognition and further development of sport science.

Representatives of sport science have been co-operating in all sections of German sport: as members in working groups and commissions of the DSB, in the governing boards and teaching groups of sport associations on the federal level, and of state sport federations, and other member organisations of the DSB.

The status and development of sport science, however, are in real danger today. The main reason is, that the personnel and material basis of sport science is linked mainly to physical education teacher training; this professional training will or shall be reduced at some universities due to many unemployed physical education teachers. This has severe consequences for sport science, and especially for the research dimension. They include:

- Discontinued funding of sport science equipment to a great extent;
- Limited grants for sport science research projects;
- Abolishment of research positions, especially for young researchers.

The consequence for sport science is, that the possibilities for doing research on topics that are important to the world of sport are being limited exactly at the time where sport science would have the scientific capacity to solve these important problems. This is contradictory to the constantly increasing importance of sport in many areas of society.

The governing body of the DSB requests from all relevant partners, especially from the Federal States, to

- keep the present number and size of sport science institutes.
- secure the present personnel- and material level of the sport science institutes.

Only then will sport science also be able in the future to deal scientifically with the manifold tasks of sport in schools, recreation, sport for all, and top-level athletics.

The governing board of the president's council of the DSB is strongly requesting to support these needs of sport science".

(3b) International: Importance of and Support for Sport Science (UNESCO 1988) (HAAG, KIRSCH & KINDERMANN 1991, 201)

The "International Council of Sport Science and Physical Education" (ICSSPE) is closely co-operating with UNESCO. In 1976 UNESCO organised - on advice of ICSSPE - the first world conference of sport ministers in Paris. In 1988 at the second conference in Moscow recommendation No 7 entitled "Importance of and Support for Sport Science" was accepted by the conference as a proposal of ICSSPE.

The Conference,

Acknowledging the importance of the application of science to the improvement of human endeavours,

Considering that study and research must precede any definition of the role of physical education and sports in the development of the individual and society,

Considering the impressive development of sport science in the past 25 years,

Recognising the contributions of sport science research to our knowledge of the influence of physical activities on individuals and society at large,

Emphasising that technological advances which improve human performance should be accessible to all,

Invites Member States:

1. to give increased support to scientific research in the field of physical education and sport;

2. to encourage institutions specialising in physical education and sport to intensify their efforts to develop sport science research and to secure the application of research results;
3. to undertake, on a regional or international basis, joint studies in the field of physical education and sport on various relevant research topics; Recommends that the Director-General of Unesco:
4. encourage effective co-operation between national and international sport science organisations;
5. foster the settingup of international exchange programs which facilitate contacts between students and scholars of sport science of all nations;
6. offer particular assistance for the establishment of sport science research centres in developing countries.

The comparative approach in sport science research - used here within the status-quo or present-day dimension - is relatively difficult and timeconsuming. Nevertheless, its importance will continue to increase in the near future. This is due to the fact, that more and more small nations are emerging, mostly on the basis of socio-cultural identity. Therefore, it will be even more important to understand other cultures and to be better prepared for new multi-cultural societies by means of studies undertaken with this comparative approach.

1.4. Futuristic Dimension

The following statements and proposals have hypothetical character, since they are projections into the future. When thinking about the future, one is never completely free from historical considerations (see 1.1); the experiences made in other countries also influence considerations regarding the future (see 1.2). Finally, the present status (see 1.3) is often the starting point for projections to the future either in confirming or changing present conditions (HEINEMANN & BECKER 1986). Therefore, ideas for the futuristic dimension are possibly generating hypotheses, which could be examined in research projects in order to make a contribution towards the development of the scientific theory in general and meta-theory of sport science in specific. The question of aims, objectives, and functions always has a final dimension rather than a causal one. Answers to the causal question, however, are often the starting point for considerations in regard to the futuristic dimension with statements of a final nature (GRUPE 1986).

Five points are mentioned, which have consequences for the futuristic dimension.

(a) The continuous **enlargement of sport as a social phenomenon** (compare 4.1) has as a consequence, that sport science must cover more and more aspects of sport. This is necessary, if sport science is taking its social responsibility serious, namely to provide scientifically gained knowledge on all aspects of sport (comprehensive approach) (HEINEMANN & BECKER 1986; DSB 1986-1988).

(b) Since movement, play, and sport are typical **international phenomena**, sport science will have the function to also become more and more international; this means, that research results should be exchanged, information on developments in regard to research methodology in sport science, given co-operative research projects planned, and more cross-cultural-international research undertaken. This has become necessary, because more and more culturally defined units, are emerging and more multicultural societies are developing (LOWE, KANIN & STRENK 1978).

(c) The so-called "Wissenschaftsethik" **(ethics of science)** has to be recognised to a greater extent in the future. This relates to the individual ethical obligations of every scientist as well as to the directing and regulating of science, which has a responsibility to the public. Since the consequences of science in general and sport science in specific are constantly increasing and since it is often not easy to calculate and foresee the outcome of the application of research results, the responsibility of the scientist for his/her research is also increasing (WILLIMCZIK 1989; NITSCH 1989).

(d) Since **research methodology** has become increasingly sophisticated and diversified it will be a major function of sport science to train especially young scientists in a very extensive way, so that they will be able to meet the standards of the world of science and to investigate issues from the field of sport, which are becoming more and more complex. In order to achieve this an extended dialogue of sport science with other scientific fields will be necessary in order to meet the request for integrated and interdisciplinary approaches (BAUERSFELD 1987; CLARKE & CLARKE 1970; HAAG 1983; HAAG 1991b; STRAUß & HAAG 1994).

(e) Dealing with aspects of philosophy of science **(meta-theory)** in general (SEIFFERT & RADNITZKY 1989) and for sport science in specific will be a function of sport science, which will become more significant in the future. This is especially important for a "young" science with a short history; it is, however, also important in order to become, be, and remain a wellinformed and constructive member of the scientific community. Only a scientific- or meta-theory based scientific discipline can meet the challenges of the future for science in a world, which is becoming increasingly complex, diversified and fast changing (LIEBER 1988; WILLIMCZIK 1968, 1979, 1980, 1987).

In five directions - **phenomenon of sport/internationality/ethics of science/research methodology/scientific theory** - a greater interest and involvement is required from sport scientists in the future. In these directions the function of sport science (its aims and objectives) are implicitly or explicitly explained. It can be stated, that all of these functions indicate that a multiple increased responsibility of sport science can be predicted in this futuristic dimension.

This may become even clearer, if future aspects in regard to the function of sport science are analysed in a further step along a research-logic model (FRIEDRICHS 1976) with the three steps: (I) discovering the research question, (II) realizing the research procedure, and (III) applying the research results.

I. **Discovery phase - finding the research question**: In the future it will be even more necessary to devote enough time and energy to this stage, i.e. to the generating of useful and justifiable research questions. Some **current deficiencies** may support this request for the future: (1) lack of theory-driven procedures in finding research questions; (2) lack of co-operation with the relevant practical fields in order to generate assumptions/hypotheses according to social needs; (3) lack of competency regarding logic research procedures, i.e. frequently a technique of data collection (e.g. an available fitness test) is the start for a research project rather than an appropriate research question; (4) lack of information on completed or ongoing research often leads to undue duplication of research. Thus it is understandable that sport science has the responsibility to employ a correct and justifiable process of generating assumptions (theoretical-hermeneutic research) or hypotheses (empirical-analytical research). The correctness and solidity of this generating phase is a first prerequisite for a high quality of sport science research.

II. **Realisation phase - carrying out the research project:** For this second part of a logic research process it will be necessary in the future to apply more sophisticated research methods, research designs, techniques of data collection, and techniques of data analysis. Many new developments in general research methodology are published. The various publications put out by the Sage Company (England) or by Pergamon Press (compare KEEVES 1989) give a good insight into the discussion led at the international level. This discussion goes beyond disciplinary considerations, since many aspects of research methodology are not bound to or applicable in only one science. Examples for such **innovations** which have to be recognised and implemented by sport science to a greater extent are: Meta analysis, triangulation, multivariate statistical analysis, probabilistic test theory, objective hermeneutics, qualitative research. These aspects only can be named in this context. It becomes clear that the place of carrying out a research project in the future will provide more challenges to the researcher due to the increasing sophistication of the available research methodology. The function of sport science therefore is to recognise and also to support this development (STRAUß 1990).

III. **Application phase - applying the research results under controlled conditions (evaluation research):** The requirement to apply research results is not new. The gap between theory and practice always has been of great concern. The **"practice to theory and theory to practice"** paradigm has difficulties in being accepted. The practitioners often complain about the researchers and vice versa. This gap has to be closed. There is an intensive transfer discussion going on in the world of science. Considerations on this topic are included in chapter 4 ("Transfer of knowledge in sport science. Or: What is the practice-theory and theory-practice paradigm"). The requirement for **evaluation research** in connection with the application of research results meets the futuristic dimension. This means, research should accompany the application of research results and find out about the consequences of the application phase. In connection with this request a relatively new development within the world of science will occur in the future, especially with technical sciences: estimating the consequences of research results application. This requirement has been put forward since some research results had very detrimental consequences for human mankind (e.g., research results used in war machinery, research results destroying nature and environment). The quest for transfer of knowledge gained in science thus is intensified; this means, that this transfer is also a target of research, namely evaluation research. This also should be seen as a major function of sport science in the future.

Having presented **five aspects** in which a **more intensive work of sport scientists** has to take place and having outlined how the **three major phases** (discovery, realisation, application) of a **logic research process** have to be viewed differently in the future; the presented futuristic dimension in regard to the issue "scientific - or meta-theory of sport science" cannot be complete; it will always have the character of perspectives and proposals.

Conclusion

In light of the title "Aims and objectives of sport science. Or: What is the function of sport science?" a very common and useful pattern of **four dimensions for scientific inquiry** has been used.

Historical - comparative - status quo - futuristic are the four dimensions, explained in their mutual relationship in the following figure:

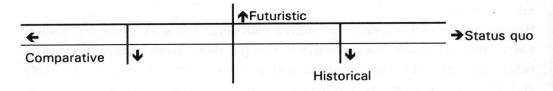

Fig. 5:   Relationship of Four Scientific Inquiry - Dimensions (HAAG)

The **historical dimension** is quite common, sometimes favoured, sometimes refused, in some cases overdone, in other cases neglected. However, the relationship of past-present-future is a basic paradigm of thinking, which can and should not be overlooked: knowing the past, understanding the present, and shaping the future. Movement, play, and sport as a part of human culture have a very interesting and exciting history. A relatively objective way to attain data under the historical perspective is to relay on key documents concerning the given topic. By analysing these in chronological order, trends and developments can be followed up to the present situation, as done in this analysis for the time span between 1955 and 1985 in an exemplary way.

The **comparative dimension** is another source for gaining as much information as possible regarding a given topic, presented in this analysis with the example of the USA. Again, this is very interesting in regard to movement, play, and sport, since these are experiences of human acting, which are bound culturally and thus provide a great variety of information. The comparative dimension as seen on a horizontal line can be applied on the vertical line in combination with historical periods, which makes this comparative approach even more attractive. With the world becoming more diversified and linked together the cross-cultural and international approach continuously is gaining importance, especially since movement, play, and sport as non-verbal human expressions are international by nature.

If the historical and comparative dimension would not be used for generating information on the given topic, it is quite understandable that the status-quo or present-day dimension has to be considered. Two parameters have been used to follow this **status-quo dimension**: Terminology in regard to sport science institutions and the development in regard to sport science organisations / sport science journals on the national and international level. There is no doubt that status-quo has to be considered as a basis for any future actions. It is also a mistake, if one remains constantly in the past or always relates to a dreamed-of so-called better future, thereby missing the present time, the actual situation, and the concrete conditions (GABLER & GÖHNER 1990).

Nevertheless, it is legitimate to look to the future. Within this **futuristic dimension** perspectives have been developed in regard to five issues, which are of basic relevance for the future development of sport science (phenomenon of sport/internationality/ethics of science/research methodology/scientific theory). Furthermore, projections have been made for three basic stages of sport science research, namely for the discovery-, realisation-, and application phase within a research process following this logical sequence. Therefore, the futuristic dimension can contribute verry much to what WILLIMCZIK (1992, 7-36) called "Interdisciplinary Sport Science - A Science in Search of its Identity".

2. The Body of Knowledge of Sport Science. Or: What is the Content of Sport Science?

Introduction

2.1. Established Theory Fields of Sport Science

    2.1.1. Sport Medicine

    2.1.2. Sport Biomechanics

    2.1.3. Sport Psychology

    2.1.4. Sport Pedagogy

    2.1.5. Sport Sociology

    2.1.6. Sport History

    2.1.7. Sport Philosophy

2.2. New Theory Fields of Sport Science

    2.2.1. Sport Information - Information Science and Sport

    2.2.2. Sport Politics - Political Science and Sport

    2.2.3. Sport Law - Science of Law and Sport

    2.2.4. Theory of Sport Facilities and Sport Equipment - Technique-Oriented Sciences and Sport

    2.2.5. Sport Economy - Economics and Sport

2.3. Sport-specific Subject Fields of Sport Science

    2.3.1. Movement Science - Movement Theory - "Bewegungslehre"

    2.3.2. Play Science - Play Theory - "Spiellehre"

    2.3.3. Training Science - Training Theory - "Trainingslehre"

    2.3.4. Instruction Science - Instruction Theory - "Unterrichtslehre" (des Sports)

2.4. General Subject Fields of Sport Science

    2.4.1. Performance and Performance Ability in Sport

    2.4.2. Music and Movement

    2.4.3. Sport and Recreation

    2.4.4. Sport and Health

    2.4.5. Sport with Special Groups

    2.4.6. Sport and Mass Media

    2.4.7. Aggression and Violence in Sport

Conclusion

Introduction

The "body of knowledge" question arises for the field of science in general and for the different scientific disciplines in specific, as for sport science. This question relates to the content of sport science and is closely linked to the development of the social subsystem of sport in its many aspects and avenues. The phenomenon of sport, in particular if one adds the aspects of movement and play as well as the educational dimensions of health education and recreation education next to movement education, has enlarged its perspectives and aspects to a great extent in recent years. This can be explained in an exemplary way, if the following model of the reality of sport is considered: professional sport, sport in state-sponsored institutions, sport in sport clubs and sport associations, sport in commercial set-ups, and private or non-institutionalised sport. Consequently, the body of knowledge of sport science constantly increases in its scope. The model for describing the body of knowledge of sport science presented in the following four steps intends to answer this new challenge of the rapidly expanding field of sport in regard to its scientific perception.

First of all, a distinction is made between theory fields and subject fields.

A theory field refers to an applied sub-discipline of a more or less established academic discipline with a relatively old history. The so-called intra-relationship between the applied sub-discipline and the academic "mother" or "relation" science is of importance within the concept of theory fields.

A subject field is considered a scientific unit which is composed of interrelationships between different theory fields related to a certain subject, which might come very directly from the field of movement, play, and sport or which might be a theme with dimensions that are not only sport-specific. Themes are considered from an interdisciplinary point of view, where a certain number of theory fields, depending on the given theme, integrate their scientific results in regard to this specific theme. These themes represent the world of sport in a very direct way, while the theory fields have a more abstract and academic discipline-oriented character.

This dual approach (theory field and subject field) to answering the question: "What is the content of sport science?" is presented in four categories for sport scientific contents, which seem to represent a static model; however it has also a dynamic character since a change within the two groups of theory fields and within the two groups of subject fields is possible. Furthermore, new fields may evolve within the historical development of a scientific discipline.

The **first category** comprises **theory fields of sport science**, which have been **in existence for some time** and which represent a considerable part of the whole body of knowledge of sport science. The following seven theory fields are considered in this first category: sport medicine, sport biomechanics, sport psychology, sport pedagogy, sport sociology, sport history and sport philosophy. These seven theory fields also represent the wide range of positions in research methodology from empirical-analytical (e.g., sport medicine) to hermeneutic-theoretical (e.g., sport philosophy).

The **second category** comprises **theory fields of sport science**, which have **only recently developed** within sport science. These are: Information science and sport - sport information; political science and sport - sport politics; jurisprudence and sport - sport law; technically oriented sciences and sport - sport facilities/ sport equipment; economics and sport - sport economics. The development of these theory fields is a direct consequence of new sport-specific professional demands, which have emerged in addition to teaching physical education and sport within and outside schools.

The **third category** comprises **subject fields of sport science**, which have a **close relationship to sport**. These are: movement theory including motor behaviour, play theory, and training theory. They are closely related to movement, play, and sport as central target points of sport science and attempt to integrate results from the theory fields in regard to the topics movement, play, and training.

The **fourth category** contains **subject fields of sport science**, which are of **relevance to sport** on one side, which, however, **also have relationships to other phenomena** and **scientific disciplines**. Examples are: performance and performance capacity in sport; music and movement; recreational sport; sport and health; adapted physical education; sport journalism; aggression/violence in sport. There are many other examples for themes at this level of abstraction (e.g., sport and aging, sport and administration, sport and environment). The examples show how far reaching the content of sport science can be. These subject fields also require the integration of interdisciplinary research results, a task that is often not easy to achieve.

With the help of these four categories it may be possible to offer a comprehensive analysis of the wide range of the body of knowledge of sport science and thus give a satisfactory answer to the question: "What is the content of sport science?"

2.1. Established Theory Fields of Sport Science

In the following a **seven-theory-field-model** is presented, which was developed in 1979 at the Department for Sport Pedagogy of the Institute of Sport and Sport Sciences, Christian-Albrechts-University at Kiel (HAAG 1979). It served as a model for describing the content of sport science (compare "review of literature") and provided part of the theoretical framework for the five-volume series "Foundations for the Study of Sport Science" edited by HAAG & STRAUß (HAAG, STRAUß & HEINZE 1989; HAAG & HEIN 1990, HAAG 1991a; STRAUß & HAAG 1994).

The seven theory fields are: **sport medicine** (HOLLMANN 1989), **sport biomechanics** (BALLREICH 1989), **sport psychology** (HAHN 1989), **sport pedagogy** (HAAG 1989b), **sport sociology** (HEINEMANN 1989a), **sport history** (LANGENFELD 1989), **sport philosophy** (HAAG 1989c). This list was created on the basis of logical considerations. The sequence of theory fields begins with sport medicine and sport biomechanics which are close to the human being in its physical existance (natural science). The three following theory fields - sport psychology, sport pedagogy, sport sociology - represent the behaviour of human beings in a holistic way (social-behavioural sciences). The last two theory fields, sport history and sport philosophy, stand for comprehensive meta-considerations in regard to past, present, and future (hermeneutical-normative sciences). Therefore, the model can be seen also as a continuum from concrete to abstract, from natural sciences to humanities, from empirical-analytical to hermeneutical-theoretical, from concrete to abstract, from descriptive to normative etc. Within the continuum of seven theory fields there are many connections and relationships. These interrelationships have to be recognised and nurtured. Furthermore, all seven theory fields have a "mother" or related discipline in the background with mostly strong interrelationships. The following figure summarises the presented characteristics of the established **seven theory fields**:

Theory Field	Related Science	Special Remarks
sport medicine	medicine	natural sciences
sport biomechanics	biology / physics	
sport psychology	psychology	social-behavioural
sport pedagogy	pedagogy	sciences
sport sociology	sociology	
sport history	history	hermeneutical-normative
sport philosophy	philosophy	sciences

Fig. 6: Seven-Theory-Field-Model (HAAG 1979, 1989a)

This model can be understood better, if each theory field is presented briefly with reference to the following points (HAAG 1991a, 119-162):

-- **Sport under the perspective of the respective theory field.**
-- **Description of the theory field.**
-- **Examples for major content areas.**
-- **Definition of the theory field by a noted scholar working in the field.**

2.1.1. Sport Medicine

Sport is the realisation of movement bound by certain anatomical and physiological preconditions. Sport is made possible in its various forms by the movement apparatus (bones, muscles, ligaments, joints) as well as the circulatory and respiratory system. Sport viewed under this perspective has a positive effect, since it improves and maintains health. Negative sides are sport-related injuries and illnesses.

Sport medicine is, on the one hand, a special area of applied medicine, and on the other hand a theory field of sport science. Within sport medicine the consequences of sportive actions (movement and non-movement) in regard to the human organism are investigated and examined with physiological and clinical methods. Furthermore, sport medicine provides support for surveying training and realizing competitions. Sport medicine deals with sport injuries; in regard to sport accidents preventive, therapeutic, and rehabilitative actions are investigated and applied. Theoretical (research) and practical (application) aspects are in close connection.

The following **issues** are example terms representing the body of knowledge of **sport medicine**: bones, muscles, nerves, cardiac and circulatory system, breathing, nutrition, energy, sensory system, sport and illness, sport under extreme conditions, hygiene and sport, sport for the handicapped, sport-medical examinations. These aspects clearly show how broad the theory field of sport medicine is.

HOLLMANN (1983, 350) defines **sport medicine** in the following way:

"Striving of theoretical and practical medicine to analyse the influence of movement, training, and sport as well as the one of lack of movement on healthy and sick individuals of all ages, and to provide knowledge about prevention, therapy, and rehabilitation. ... In Germany and in many other countries sport medicine is recognised as an independent area for research, teaching, and practice. ... The most important social significance of sport medicine is its role within preventive medicine and rehabilitation". In the German language sport medicine is used in a comprehensive way; it includes the English terms like exercise physiology, biochemistry, and sport medicine.

For **further information** on the theory field of **sport medicine** compare the following sources: HAAG & HEIN 1990, 80-90, 402-404; HOLLMANN 1989, 6-17 - the same in English: HOLLMANN 1992, 105-118; BÖHMER 1984b, 233-258 and 941-951; de MARÉES, 1984, 92-104; HOLLMANN 1980, 316-347; BERG & KEUL 1992, 37-68; URHAUSEN & KINDERMANN 1992, 69-104; ROST 1992, 119-146.

2.1.2. Sport Biomechanics

Sport is a form of human movement which can be developed in an optimal way by adequate procedures of learning, exercising, and training. Biological and mechanical lawlike aspects play a major role for the execution of movements.

Sport biomechanics is a theory field of sport science that deals with movement as one behavioural dimension of men. With the help of very differentiated techniques of data collection movements are examined; the results can be used for the development of optimal technique solutions in sport.

The following **issues** are examples representing the body of knowledge of **sport biomechanics**:

movement description (motor patterns), explanation of applied forces, biomechanical parameters for condition and coordination, analysis and improvement of skills in different sports, biomechanical aids for learning, exercising and training, demands on the movement apparatus, designing sport facilities and equipment, development of biomechanical theories (principles and laws) and measurement procedures.

BAUMANN (1983, 79-80) defines **sport biomechanics** in the following way:

"The content of sport biomechanics is the human body and the sportive movement. Tasks are the objective, quantitative description and explanation of reality ... by using to a great extent the language of mathematics. The used measurement techniques are biomechanical anthropometry, kinemetry, dynamometry, and electromyography ... Basic mechanical parameters are time, distance, mass; derived parameters are, e.g.: velocity, force, impulse, torque, work, energy, power. Biological foundations are given by the structure and function of the passive movement apparatus. ... Based on those foundations ... biomechanical principles are formulated, thus allowing a judgement on the efficiency of movements. ...Criteria for optimisation: ... Minimising energy consumption, minimising strain on the movement apparatus, reducing the performance challenge for the movement apparatus, maximising of muscle output. ... Biomechanical measurement techniques can be differentiated according to the type of parameters measured: ... Kinematic ... dynamometric. ... According to the measurement principle one can distinguish: mechanical ..., electronic ... optical measurement techniques."

For **further information** on the theory field of **sport biomechanics** compare the following sources: HAAG & HEIN 1990, 90-92, 404-405; BALLREICH 1989, 18-29 - the same in English: BALLREICH 1992, 147-162; BRÜGGEMANN 1984, 259-302; REISCHLE & SPIKERMANN 1992, 163-190.

2.1.3. Sport Psychology

Sport comprises several dimensions of human acting and behavior, where motor, cognitive, and affective components play a role, and which result in the production of many different movement patterns.

Sport psychology deals as applied and special psychology and as theory field of sport science with different aspects of human sport-related behaviour. This relates to causes and preconditions, process structures, experiences as well as results and socially implicit relationships of movement behaviour in sport. A system of sport psychology can be seen under three perspectives: (1) psychology of different sports such as, e.g. swimming, (2) psychology of different sport areas, e.g. top-level athletics, (3) psychology of basic behaviour patterns in sport, e.g. psychology of play.

The following **issues** are examples representing the body of knowledge of **sport psychology**: action psychology and sport training and competition in sport, aspects of sport psychology of sport disciplines; talent in sport; sport and personality; motor development; motor learning; motor control; aspects of social psychology; movement therapy and movement education; motivational psychology; diagnosis of cognitive and affective aspects of performance in sport.

GABLER (1983, 353-355) defines **sport psychology** as follows:

"Sport psychology attempts to register human behaviour and experience in the practical field of sport as precisely as possible. This means the following: to describe constancy and change and, if possible, to measure it; to define the prerequisites for constancy and change and to predict, if possible, the future process. ... The main aspects of current research and literature in sport psychology are in the field of learning and developmental psychology, motivation and personality psychology as well as social psychology. ... Besides teaching and producing research sport psychologists have become increasingly involved with counselling top-level athletes... . In light of these tasks and activities it makes sense to characterise sport psychology as a relatively independent part of psychology; one can describe its internal structure by means of three categories of specific activities: psychology-related and non-research-oriented activities (counselling of athletes); psychological-technological innovative- (research) activities (development of a tennis-test); psychological-scientific innovative-(research) activities (problem solving theory for behaviour in skiing). ... In regard to the relationship of sport psychology to sport science ... additional levels of scientific work can be distinguished: disciplinary orientation; ... interdisciplinary-additive orientation; ... interdisciplinary-integrative orientation."

For **further information** on the theory field of **sport psychology** compare the following sources: HAAG & HEIN 1990, 93-102, 405-406; HAHN 1989, 36-47; SIMONS 1984, 497-585; UNGERER-RÖHRICH & SINGER 1984, 5-19; GABLER & RÖTHIG 1980, 111-141; NITSCH 1992, 263-296; SCHWENKMEZGER & RIEDER 1992, 297-328.

2.1.4. Sport Pedagogy

Sport is a form of human movement behaviour, for which and through which one can educate.

Sport pedagogy is on one side special and applied pedagogy and on the other side theory field of sport science. It deals with functional (unintended) and intentional (planned) possibilities and limitations of education for and through movement, play, and sport. Sport pedagogy deals with teaching and learning of all age groups, without discrimination in regard to sex, race, religion or socio-economic status. Teaching and learning inside and outside of state institutions are studied. Target groups for sport pedagogy are individuals with a low level of performance (e.g., adapted physical education groups) as well as individuals who are talented and motivated for engagement in top-level athletics (e.g., training groups). Curriculum theory of sport on one side and instruction theory of sport on the other side provide information for developing an optimal educational practice oriented towards movement play, and sport from a theoretical point of view (HAAG 1982a; 1986b; 1987b; 1989d).

The following **issues** are examples representing the body of knowledge of **sport pedagogy**: historical perspective of sport pedagogy; self-understanding and nature of sport pedagogy; anthropological foundations; curriculum theory of sport; instruction theory of sport; comparative aspects of sport pedagogy.

GRUPE & KURZ (1983, 351-352) define **sport pedagogy** as follows:

"The science ..., which is concerned with the relationship between sport and education. There is agreement that sport pedagogy should provide theoretical foundations for the practice of sport; this practice is educational, supports human development, and enriches life. ... Furthermore, the fact that people can learn and develop themselves throughout their life, ... requires that adults, seniors, and handicapped people should be included in the issues of sport pedagogy. ... Sport pedagogy has to view sport in a broader context of the meaning of movement, body, play, performance, health, and leisure-time for the human being, ... Therefore, work in education has to consider, e.g., the various unplanned and rather hidden socialisation influences on the attitudes towards body, movement, play, and sport."

For **further information** on **sport pedagogy** compare the following sources: HAAG & HEIN 1990, 103-125, 407-410; HAAG 1989b, 48-69 - the same in English: HAAG 1992a, 329-360; PREISING 1984, 23-62; KAYSER 1984a, 63-82; GRUPE 1980b, 216-243; SCHMITZ 1980, 244-266; RIEDER & SCHMIDT 1980, 267-315; GRUPE 1992, 361-378.

2.1.5. Sport Sociology

Sport is a central social phenomenon, which is shaped by many socio-cultural factors.
Sport Sociology is on one side special and applied sociology and on the other side theory field of sport science. It is the aim of sport sociology to investigate the action field sport in regard to its internal structure and position in society (external structure). This includes questions of micro-sociology like group behaviour, but also macro-sociological issues like the organisational structure of a national sport system. Three areas can be distinguished according to HEINEMANN (1990): preconditions of sport and engaging in sport from the point of view of action theory; social structures in sport and sport groups; relation between sport and society. Sport sociology utilises a wide range of ways to gain knowledge, from theoretical-hermeneutical up to empirical-analytical.
The following **issues** are examples representing the body of knowledge of **sport sociology**: sport and society; sport and major activities of human life (daily routine, work, leisure time); sport and social fields; sport under the aspect of institutions/organisations; sport in the context of individual sociology; sport and socialisation; sport and social problems; sport in intercultural comparison.
HEINEMANN (1983, 358-359) defines **sport sociology** as follows:

"Sport sociology is special sociology as well as special sport science. ... Therefore, sport sociology deals with this action field sport in the following directions:
internal structure; position within different forms of society; its functional and
symbolic meaning etc. Sport sociology is also special sport science by dealing
with specific problems of sport and by striving to find solutions for current
problems in this action field by following synthetical approaches in cooperation
with other sciences. ... Sport sociology 1. a sociology of social systems. ... a.
the manifold determinations and influences of sport from cultural value systems
and socio-structural conditions in a society ... .b. the social structures and
processes within sport ... . c. influences of sport on individuals, on social areas
like family, work place, politics, church, educational system, and on the social
structure in total. ... The sociology of sport is 2. sociology of "social figures".
... The sports person, coach, referee, official etc. can be the target of research
in sport sociology as a "social figure". ... Sport sociology is 3. sociology of related issues and determinations along subject matter lines."

For **further information** on **sport sociology** compare the following sources:
HAAG & HEIN 1990, 125-134, 411; HEINEMANN 1989a, 70-81 - the same in
English: HEINEMANN 1992a, 379-402; ANDERS 1984a, 193-231; RITTNER,
MRAZEK & LAMMERSDORF 1984, 48-61; HAMMERICH & LÜSCHEN 1980,
183-214; HEINEMANN 1992b, 403-422.

2.1.6. Sport History

Sport is a social phenomenon which is historically developed and changes constantly. In its present form, as a total unit or in aspects like callisthenics, gymnastics, play, dance, etc.; it can be understood better on the basis of its historical development.
Sport history is on one side special history and on the other side theory field of
sport science. Sport history deals with the presentation and explanation of the
development of sport, with physical activity and physical education in a broad
sense. Sport history attempts to analyse and explain the past; based on this it
develops an objective and rational presentation, explanation, and interpretation
of the present situation of movement, play, and sport. Finally, historical knowledge should contribute to influence the future development of sport in a reasonable way.
The following **issues** are examples representing the body of knowledge of **sport
history**: Greek antiquity; Roman antiquity; physical activity in the middle ages;
the time of enlightenment (1680-1800); history of movement, callisthenics,

gymnastics, play, and sport; reform pedagogy (beginning of the 20th century); sport and physical activity under the NS regime (1933-1945); contemporary history of sport (1945 until today).

BECKER & LANGENFELD (1983, 345-346) define **sport history** in the following way:

"Sport history is part of sport science, but in principle also of general historical science; it deals with research and presentation of historical forms of physical activities, of historical systems of physical education (of all people and times), and of their ideological, organisational, and institutional development. ... Within the Federal Republic of Germany an attempt was made (after 1945) to conceptualise sport history as culture, motive, universal, problem and recently also as structural history with the aim to overcome an understanding of history, which has been predominantly chronological. ... In the German Democratic Republic the concept of history was developed on the basis of dialectic and historical materialism in line with the communist party and its dogmatism; this was a history of physical culture which saw it as a social-political phenomenon in close relation to the development of productivity. ... Within sport history the schemes dividing history into periods should not be oriented solely on data of political history, but rather should consider the conditions of the social, economic, cultural, and human developments and their mutual relationships."

For **further information** on **sport history** compare the following sources: HAAG & HEIN 1990, 134-144, 412-413; LANGENFELD 1989, 82-93 - the same in English: LANGENFELD 1992, 423-438; WOLF 1984, 795-820; BERNETT 1984, 20-27; BEGOV 1980, 24-28; BERNETT 1980, 59-87; BERNETT 1992, 439-462.

2.1.7. Sport Philosophy

Sport is a complex form of human life which can be explained under the perspective of the following sub disciplines of general philosophy: anthropology, ontology, cultural philosophy, aesthetics, ethics, and scientific theory. Sport is a certain way of being, in which man is actualising the body through movement, by which a diversity of actions is produced. Thus, sport has become a phenomenon with large existential variety in regard to the possibilities for self-realization of human life.

Sport philosophy is on one side special and applied philosophy and on the other side theory field of sport science. Sport philosophy deals especially with research on the philosophical preconditions and interpretations of sport in its different forms of realisation. Sport philosophy also contributes to the scientific foundation of the theory fields or sub disciplines of sport science. Sport philosophy can be considered an applied philosophy, dealing with central phenomena of society, e.g., as is done in religious, art, economic, and state philosophy. Like the theory field of sport history (retrospective), sport philosophy produces a more prospective work and thus provides a necessary comprehensive analysis and reflection of sport in its different forms as a central social phenomenon.

The following **issues** are examples representing the body of knowledge of **sport philosophy**: scientific theory of sport science; anthropology (body); philosophy of performance in sport; philosophy of play; aesthetics and sport; social philosophy of sport; ethics and sport; movement philosophy (kinephilosophy).

LENK (1983, 282-283) defines **sport philosophy** in the following way:

"Philosophy is interpreting sport as individual and social phenomenon as well as educational field coming from different philosophical frameworks: philosophical anthropology, aesthetics, existential philosophy, life-philosophy, phenomenology, social philosophy, and cultural philosophy. ... The investigation of the following topics belongs to the tasks of sport philosophy: philosophical foundation of sport pedagogy; analysis of sport science from the point of view of scientific theory; development of a general philosophical action theory especially of the behaviour oriented towards performance and physical challenge. The philosophy of sport is a new discipline and has only developed during the last ten years when the question was asked quite often. What is the justification for (e.g., also sport). ... It is a new line of work to combine the traditional and modern orientations on social-philosophical interpretations. ... From a methodological point of view philosophy employs predominantly phenomenological methods ... . During the last years multicategorial parameters were used more and more. They included aspects of humanistic, behavioural, or sport science. ... Methods of analytical action philosophy, of semiotics and scientific theory still await recognition by sport philosophy."

For **further information** on **sport philosophy** compare the following sources: HAAG & HEIN 1990, 145-148, 413-414; HAAG 1989c, 94-123 - the same in English: HAAG 1992b, 463-500; CARL u.a. 1984, 3-19; GRUPE 1984a, 79-91; GRUPE 1980c, 11-22; GRUPE 1980a, 88-110; FRANKE 1992, 501-536.

With these **seven theory fields**, presented in their basic **aim, content, and struc-ture** a large part of the body of knowledge of sport science can be described and explained.

The next major categories described below will add to the body of knowledge and make it clear that the grouping, number, and relevance of theory fields of sport science is constantly changing according to the needs of social reality.

2.2. New Theory Fields of Sport Science

In the following **five new theory fields** are presented, which have been developed recently especially since about 1980 in a more scientific manner. This is also due to the fact that the significance of sport as a social phenomenon has increased tremendously, and that it has become a relevant factor in our society. Consequently, more and more dimensions of human life play an important role in connection with sport.

These five new theory fields of sport science also provide part of the theoretical framework for the five-volume series "Foundations for the Study of Sport Science" edited by HAAG & STRAUß (HAAG, STRAUß & HEINZE 1989; HAAG & HEIN 1990; HAAG 1991a; STRAUß & HAAG 1994).

The **five new theory fields** are: **information science and sport - sport information** (KNEYER 1989); **political science and sport - sport politics** (GÜLDENPFENNIG 1989); **science of law and sport - sport law** (RESCHKE 1989); **technically oriented sciences and sport - theory of sport facilities and sport equipment** (ROSKAM 1989); **economics and sport - sport economy** (HEINEMANN 1989b). The given sequence of these five theory fields is according to the alphabet in German and not according to logic consideration.

All five theory fields are closely interrelated and also related to the seven theory fields in chapter 2.1. Furthermore, all of them have a "mother" - or "related" science in the background with strong interrelationships.

The following figure summarises the presented characteristics of the five new theory fields of sport science.

Theory Field	Related Science	Special Remarks
sport information	information science	increasing information with more and more importance
sport politics	political science	sport as social phenomenon has political aspects
sport law	law	increasing of administration and bureaucratisation
sport facilities - sport equipment	architecture, engineering	disregarded for a long time, but important
sport economy	economics	economy as the "new" ideology of sport

Fig. 7: Five-Theory-Field-Model (HAAG 1979, 1989a)

This model can be understood better, if each theory field is presented briefly with reference to the following points (HAAG 1991a, 163-196):

-- **Sport under the perspective of the respective theory field.**
-- **Description of the theory field.**
-- **Examples for major content areas.**
-- **Definition of the theory field by a noted scholar working in the field.**

In science in general and in sport science in specific the rapidity of developments is constantly increasing. Therefore it is likely that one or another of these five new theory fields will develop in the future to an extent, that it can be included in the seven-theory-field-model (see 2.1) Similarly, new theory fields are originating and thus changing the five-theory-field-model. In other words, a flexible and dynamic model for the description of the body of knowledge of sport science with an orientation towards theory fields or disciplines as developed in this study is necessary.

This model can be understood better, if each theory field is presented briefly with reference to the following points (HAAG 1991a, 119-162).
— **Sport under the perspective of the respective theory field.**
— **Description of the theory field.**
— **Examples for major content areas.**
— **Definition of the theory field by a noted scholar working in the field.**

2.2.1. Sport Information - Information Science and Sport

Sport is part of the social life, and is realised in many forms. It has become an important part of the information system next to politics, economics and culture. This becomes evident in various publications, from newspaper up to TV. Sport as part of human life constantly produces information which is relayed to others and documented. Sport has to be viewed as a generator of information.

Sport information or **information science and sport** is on one side an applied part of information science and on the other side a theory field of sport science. Sport information as a theory field has developed quite rapidly in recent years due to the huge amount of information on sport in its different aspects. The process of receiving, storing, and retrieving information requires that strategies and models of information science are designed in regard to sport; this task is achieved by a sport-related information science. Documentation plays an important role in this process, considering different dimensions of data such as documents, literature, and audio-visual material. Information science itself is an integrative science consisting of parts of traditional sciences like linguistics, politics, psychology, sociology, and technology; these aspects are also relevant for sport information science, thus requiring a high degree of integrative thinking within sport information.

According to KNEYER (1989, 126-137) the following **issues** are examples representing the body of knowledge of **sport information**: information linguistics, information politics, information psychology, information sociology, information technology and information norming.

SCHMITZ (1983, 108-109) defines **documentation** as a basic term for information in the following way:

"Structured collection of data and documents of all kinds, including content analysis and treatment through systematisation, classification, selection, analysis, and writing a summary. Documentation serves the fast and complete information on a topic, issue, or scientific problem. One has to distinguish between primary documentation (... original documents ...) and secondary documentation (bibliographies ...). Importance and range of documentation. ... The systematic elements of documentation (description, retrieval, classification) and the necessary special knowledge support a tendency that documentation is becoming a scientific field in its own right. ...

The "International Association of Sport Information" is responsible for documentation in sport.

Within the German speaking countries the **following documentation centres** exist: Cologne (BISp - Federal Institute of Sport Science); Leipzig (IAT - Institute for Applied Science of Coaching and Training); Vienna (Austrian Documentation and Information Centre for Sport); Magglingen, Suisse (ETSS -Library)."

For **further information** on **sport information** compare the following sources: HAAG & HEIN 1990, 149-190, 415-416; KNEYER 1989, 126-137.

2.2.2. Sport Politics - Political Science and Sport

Sport is as sub-system of society closely related to strategies for political logic. On the one hand, sport is influenced by politics in regard to its possibilities; on the other hand, sport is also an instrument of politics and in danger of being used for political purposes (ideology).

Sport politics serves as a term for every sport-oriented public action of individuals as well as institutions. Sport actions are realised between sport as a social force with relative independence and the state as an institution which is responsible for organising public life. Both poles, sport and politics, are sometimes seen too absolute. As a consequence, sport is viewed with respect to sport politics either as a politically free room or as a means of politics. The possibilities for sport politic action between these two poles are unfortunately, not recognised very often. Reasonable action-oriented sport politics are in danger, if sport misuses politics (e.g., exaggerated demands from the state to build large sport facilities or overlooking environmental guidelines when practising sports) or if politics misuse sport (e.g., boycott of the Olympic Games or sport as means of nationalistic presentation). Domestic and foreign action is the case of sport politics. In Germany this is realised by two partners: public sports administration and self-administration of sport, which both exist on four levels: community, state, federal, and international.

The term sport politics also stands for the theoretical and scientific dealing with problems of sport politics as explained before. This is done within the theory field "sport politics" (sport politology) of sport science in close cooperation with sport sociology.

According to GÜLDENPFENNIG (1989, 173-175) the following **issues** are examples representing the body of knowledge of **sport politics**: parts of the sport system; institutions and organisations of the sport system; people responsible for action in the sport system; sport-political actions; social interests in the sport system; plans and programs in regard to sport politics; sport-political events; sport-political ideas; sport politics as social politics; sport politics as form of political culture; sport politics as educational politics; influences of sport politics on the sport and social system.

BLOSS (1983b, 352-353) defines **sport politics** in the following way: "The two contrary positions 'sport as means of politics' and 'sport as politically free room' must be recognised. Furthermore, the relationship of sport and politics can be seen in two ways:

(1) sport politics is planning and deciding in regard to domestic and foreign politics, which are related to sport in a broader sense. These are actions of the federal, state, and local level (public sport administration) as well as of social groups and institutions (self-administration of sport), which comprise tasks, functions and objectives of the so-called free, organised and institutionalised sport. Sport is therefore defined through the headway given by politics. Sport is not autonomous and not action independent of the total society; rather, sport has a mutual relationship to politics.

(2) Sport politics in a more narrow sense is a theory field of sport science, sometimes also seen as part of sport sociology. As sport politology the following issues are within this scientific responsibility: sport and social politics; sport and political parties; sport and institutions; sport in foreign politics and in the international world".

For **further information** on **sport politics** compare the following sources: HAAG & HEIN 1989, 150-154, 416-417; GÜLDENPFENNIG 1989, 238-259; WOLF 1984, 795-819; ANDERS 1984b, 821-839; HAMMERER 1984, 841-876; HAAG, KIRSCH & KINDERMANN 1991.

2.2.3. Sport Law - Science of Law and Sport

Sport is part of the society which is characterized by an increasing influence of laws and regulations depending on the degree of being bound in an organisation. The degree of regulation is high in professional sport, with a decreasing tendency from sport in federal education institutions, club sport, commercialised sport, to non-institutionalised sport. Sport as subsystem of society thus is more and more characterized by laws and regulations.

Two forms can be distinguished in regard to aspects of sport law:

(1) The self-administration of sport has its own law system, especially laws related to sport clubs and sport associations; special non-state law courts exist to support these laws.

(2) Sport law as the sum of laws, which can be applied to sport. These are especially the following law sections, partly related to the public sport administration:

Regulations and laws related to sport disciplines, which touch areas of public authority. Examples are: aeronautical sports (law for air traffic); water sports (law for marine traffic); winter sports (environmental law); school sports (school law); the liability law to regulate the legal responsibility between a sport club and its members, the company and its employees in industry sport; people organising sport events and participating athletes as well as spectators. Sport law has an increasing importance; the more sport is expanding, the larger is the role of administration and bureaucracy and the greater is the economic influence on the respective area of sport.

According to RESCHKE (1989, 160-173) the following **issues** are examples representing the body of knowledge of **sport law**: laws related to clubs, associations, contracts, liability, insurance, work and social affairs, neighbourhood, competition, state and administration, taxes, criminal acts, and European Community regulations.

RESCHKE (1989, 160-161) defines **sport law** in the following way: "If people engage together in sport, it is necessary to have rules and accept which are valid for a game or a comparison of performance. The function of referees and judges has to be based on rules, because these persons watch over the abiding by the rules and decide on sanctions if rules are violated, which means a clearly defined disadvantage for the athlete or team who violated the rule(s). Furthermore, minimal organisational prerequisites, the right to play and participate, obligations, and rights of the participants or members must be defined. The basic issue of sport law is the obligation to these rules, interpretation, application and evaluation of the norms in regard to justice in sport but also their relation to general laws. Sport law in a more narrow sense is related to the norms of sport, this means statutes, orders, and regulations of clubs and associations, which organise sport. ... The free development of the personality, and this includes the free engagement in sport, are limited according to article 2 of the German Constitutional Law regarding the rights of others, the constitution and ethical norms. If personal rights, other rights or even human rights are violated, there may be requests for liability towards athletes and sport organisations; on the other hand, it is also possible that athletes and sport organisations have liability requests against others. The more sport is developing into a phenomenon related to many parts of society and the more the request for "sport for all" is supported by sport organisations, the more the general laws are part of the sport scene. Since these laws do, however, regulate special issues rather than sport directly, the relationship between sport and law, jurisdiction and the science of law has to be viewed in light of the connection between sport and law in a broad sense."

For **further information** on **sport law** compare the following sources: HAAG & HEIN 1990, 154-156; RESCHKE 1989, 160-173.

2.2.4. Theory of Sport Facilities and Sport Equipment - Technique-Oriented Sciences and Sport

Sport is a form of human movement behaviour, which is depends normally on facilities and/or equipment. This dependency also has a creative side to it, since new developments in regard to sport facilities and sport equipment may lead to the development of new technical and tactical skills in relation to motor patterns as well as totally new sport activities (e.g., paragliding, snow boarding etc.)..
The large expansion of sport disciplines ultimately is also a result of the devel-

opment of sport facilities and especially sport equipment. Consequently there is a mutual relationship between sport and sport facilities/ sport equipment.

In regard to a **theory of sport facilities and sport equipment** several aspects have to be considered. Sport and the practising of sport are bound to different material and technical prerequisites. The totality of sport forms and sport disciplines can be categorised according to these criteria: sports practiced with or without an apparatus, summer-winter, water-air, indoor-outdoor etc. The theory of sport facilities and sport equipment comprises aspects of development, producing, using, maintaining, and renewing of sport facilities and sport equipment. In competitive sport the sport facilities and sport equipment have to meet precise regulations.

The term **"sport facilities"** (sport, play, and recreation facilities) means the sum of all instalments, which serve the practice of sport and a sport-oriented use of leisure time. One differentiates between facilities used independent of sport disciplines and facilities designed especially for a certain sport discipline. Additional facilities also must be considered, such as changing rooms for the officials or rooms for the equipment.

The term **"sport equipment"** stands for the equipment used in certain sport disciplines; this equipment including sport dress and sport shoes can be seen as the necessary overall prerequisite for engaging in sport. Sport equipment can be categorised according to the following criteria: small and large equipment; equipment which is movable; equipment (apparatus) on which movement is performed; equipment which moves man; equipment for indoor and outdoor use.

According to ROSKAM (1989, 174-183) the following **issues** are examples representing the body of knowledge of the **theory of sport facilities and sport equipment**: relationship of the kind of sport facility and sport equipment and the planning phase as well as the use of the sport facility. Examples for issues related to sport facilities: heating, acoustics, possibility of injury, hygienic system, multiple usage, artificial installations. Examples for sport equipment are: sport discipline specific equipment like rowing boats, bikes, skis, tennis rackets.

ROSKAM (1983, 362-369) defines the term building of **sport facilities (including sport equipment)** in the following way:

"The expression" building of sport facilities" comprises all actions related to the planning of requests, preparation of the plan, and building of facilities for recreation, play, and sport facilities. The consequences for the servicing of the sport facilities are also included.

Within the "regulations for building recreation, play, and sport facilities" these facilities are enumerated . ... Open-air facilities close to living areas, playing fields and sport fields, sport gymnasiums, swimming pools, indoor and outdoor facilities, special facilities for certain sport disciplines, and indoor facilities in sport centres. ... Basic prerequisite for the provision of adequate facilities for the people interested in sport and sport-oriented leisure time is the analysis of the people's needs as a basis for determining the necessary facilities in different variations; this relates to facilities for play in pre-school age, for school sport, club sport (sport for all) and top-level athletics as well as for recreational sport."

For **further information** on the theory of **sport facilities and sport equipment** compare the following sources: HAAG & HEIN 1990, 156-161, 417-418; ROSKAM 1989, 174-183.

2.2.5. Sport Economy - Economics and Sport

Sport is a social area which is on the one hand influenced quite strongly by the economy, and which, on the other hand, becomes an important economic factor in different active and passive forms of sport reality. One can call the economy the new ideology of sport since it has replaced politics to a great extent in this ideology-oriented function.

Economics of sport or **sport economy** is an applied sub-discipline of economic sciences and a theory field of sport science, investigating the relationship between sport and economy. The constantly increasing commercialisation and professionalization of sport can be seen clearly in two directions:

a) Object-related support of the economy for sport, like equipment for athletes (dress, shoes, apparatus), building of sport facilities.
b) Person-related services, like administering of sport clubs, fitness-centres, sport schools; sport activity programs offered by the tourism industry; organisation of sport events for spectators.

One can interpret the area of economy or the world of business as the modern ideology of sport. This means that sport is used for various purposes of the economic system.

Sport has to be careful since it can have a major input and define the direction of the cooperation with the world of business. Therefore, the theory field of sport economy also has to deal with these general sociological and philosophical questions.

According to HEINEMANN (1989b, 184-185) the following **issues** are examples for defining the body of knowledge of **sport economy**: micro-economic topics (e.g., economic objectives of sport programs offered in commercialised settings); meso-economic topics (e.g., economy of commercialisation); macro-economic topics (e.g., sport and economic system).

BLOSS (1983a, 351) defines **sport economy** in the following way:

"Sport economy deals with all questions related to sport and economics. Until now his relationship has been investigated only to a small extent. Sport has become a major economic factor in modern industrialised societies. Billions of dollars are involved in the production of sport equipment and sport clothes, in trade with sport equipment, in the building of sport facilities, in the advertisement industry as well as in professional sport. All of this has national and international relevance for the country and the business world. Sport economy undergoes two major developments. On one side, scientific-technical inventions of sport equipment make it possible to enlarge offered recreation activities and to produce unexpected advancement of performance in top-level-athletics. On the other side, the status of the so-called amateur sportsman and sportswoman is in danger due to the influence and pressure resulting from economic interests."

For **further information** on **sport economy** compare the following sources: HAAG & HEIN 1990, 161-162, 418-419; HEINEMANN 1989b, 184-195- the same in English: HEINEMANN 1992b, 403-422; HEINEMANN 1987; HEINEMANN 1984.

2.3. Sport-Specific Subject Fields of Sport Science

In the following four **subject fields** are presented, which are in **direct relationship to movement, play, and sport**. These subject fields represent the central core of sport science. Like the theory fields (compare 2.1 and 2.2) these subject fields are part of the theoretical framework for the five-volume series "Foundations for the Study of Sport Science" edited by HAAG & STRAUß (STRAUß & HEINZE 1989; HAAG & HEIN 1990; HAAG 1991a; HAAG, STRAUß & HAAG 1994).

In connection with the terms **movement theory, play theory, training theory, and instruction theory** it has to be stated, that two other sets of terms are used, which will be mentioned briefly, in order to underline the context of the four sport-specific subject-fields of sport science.

One set is **movement science, play science, training science, and instruction science**, which name the scientific subject field; results of the work in these sciences are then integrated into **theories** in regard to **movement, play, training, and instruction**. These theories are collected, structured and presented in a form, which is geared towards realizing knowledge transfer in the areas of movement, play, and sport. The German word for this would be: (1) "Bewegungslehre" (GÖHNER 1989), (2) "Spiellehre" (GRUPE & KRÜGER 1989), (3) "Trainingslehre" (CARL 1989) and "Unterrichtslehre" (des Sports)(HAAG 1985). The first, second, and third area is developed quite extensively, the second one still needs further development.

Figure 8 summarises the mentioned terminological variations and their meaning:

Sport-specific Subject Field	Scientific Dimension	Theory Dimension	Application Dimension	Specific Remarks
movement	movement science	movement theory =	"Bewegungs- lehre"	developed to a great extent
play	play science	play theory =	"Spiellehre"	has also a non-sport dimen- sion
training	training science	training theory =	"Trainings- lehre"	including coaching
(sport) instruction	instruction science (of sport)	instruction theory (of sport) =	"Unterrichts- lehre" (des Sports)	equivalent term "sport- didactics"

Fig. 8: Three-Subject-Field-Model (HAAG 1979, 1989a)

It is not so important which of the two sets of terms (science or theory equivalent to "-lehre") is used; however, it is necessary to indicate the theoretical assumptions connected with these categories for describing the body of knowledge of sport science.

This model can be understood better, if each theme field is presented briefly with reference to the following points (HAAG 1991a, 197-219):

-- **Sport under the perspective of the respective theme field.**
-- **Description of the theme field.**
-- **Examples for major content areas.**
-- **Definition of the theme field by a noted scholar working in the field.**

The major point which distinguishes a theory field from a subject field is that the latter one originates by integrating research results (theories and knowledge) gained within the theory fields and geared towards topics like movement, play, training, or instruction. Therefore, the **paradigm** of **interdisciplinarity and integration** is applied in these subject fields.

2.3.1. Movement Science - Movement Theory - "Bewegungslehre"

Sport is one form in which human movement behaviour is realised. It can be explained according to outside signs of movement and according to inside laws of the motor system. This explanation of sport from the point of view of movement science must be very variable due to the many forms for realisation of sport; the result is a large variety of possible sport-related movement-analyses.

Movement Science comprises all the scientific approaches, which can contribute to the scientific explanation of the phenomena "movement". The interdisciplinary and integrative character of this sport-specific subject field is indicated by this definition.

Movement theory is a system of knowledge about the different meanings of movement, gained on a more or less scientific basis (1) Movement as a change of position, status or posture; (2) movement as an internal experience; (3) movement of a large group in regard to politically and/or historically important common goals. For sport, only the first meaning is of relevance.

"Bewegungslehre" means in clear consequence a systematic collection and summary of scientific knowledge (theories) on movement in sport, under the aspect of organising this knowledge in order to be applied practically. "Bewegungslehre" thus comprises the movement action in sport-related situations on the basis of results of movement research. Within "Bewegungslehre" of sport different models for analysing sport movements are presented; they have emerged from different scientific approaches or theory fields of sport science.

- sport medicine: aspects of functional anatomy and physiology.
- sport biomechanics: analyses by means of cinematography and dynamometry.
- sport psychology: sensorimotor interpretation, this means movement performance as relation of sensory input and motor output.
- sport pedagogy: model of functional phases in order to describe the aim of movement steps (phases); phenographic-morphologic description of movement to gain information regarding the correct movement realisations.
- sport sociology: socio-cultural variations of movement performance.
- sport history: historical determination and change of sport movements.
- sport philosophy: phenomenological analysis of sport movement.

Besides "Trainingslehre" (training theory)/"Bewegungslehre" (movement theory) is the most developed sport-specific subject field of sport science. It requires integrative and interdisciplinary procedures.

The following **issues** are examples for defining the body of knowledge of **movement science-movement theory = "Bewegungslehre"**:

the concept of a sport movement; movement - movement structure - "outside view" of movement (natural sciences approach); movement - movement structure - "outside view" of movement (social and behavioural sciences approach); motor behaviour - motor control - "inside view" of movement; motor development and motor learning; assessment, evaluation, and transfer of results related to sport-specific movement performances.

GÖHNER (1983, 70) defines **"Bewegungslehre"** in the following way: "'Bewegungslehre' is the sum of scientific results on the problem of movement in sport. This means the knowledge on sport movements and sportive moving, gained in the theory of physical education and in sport science research and presented in an 'Bewegungslehre'. Thus, it comprises different concepts, which are limited by certain assumptions and characterized by certain theories."

The following are **educational-normative concepts**: Theory of Austrian school gymnastics; theory of rhythmical callisthenics; educational theory of sportive movement developed by MEINEL & SCHNABEL (1987). In these concepts statements are made in regard to the entire physical activities of callisthenics and sport under a specific understanding of movement, which is educationally justified. The central points of this approach are: indication of the main characteristics of selected movements; search for and investigation of movement principles; description and instructional application of learning the relevant movements.

There is a **cybernetics-oriented concept**, in which the moving person is seen as a system dealing with information (sensorimotor system).

There are **integrative-functional concepts** (functional "Bewegungslehre"), which are characterized by gaining insight into the relationship of movement as product (motor skill) and movement as process (movement action) in traditionally given or future situations of physical activity or sport. Main aspects of a functional "Bewegungslehre" are: research on sport-specific movement problems (movement tasks); research on necessities and degrees of freedom of available and unknown solutions; analyses of individual actions to solve a problem; the particularities of motor learning during repeated problem solving.

For **further information** on **movement science-movement theory = "Bewegungslehre"** compare the following sources: GÖHNER 1992, 191-200 (English); MECHLING & ROTH 1992, 201-222 (English); HAAG & HEIN 1990, 162-171, 421; MEINEL & SCHNABEL 1987; GÖHNER 1989, 198-207; MECHLING 1984, 83-134; JOCH 1984, 353-380; DAUGS, & BLISCHKE 1984, 381-420; STARISCHKA 1984, 421-456; BÖS 1984, 457-495; GÖHNER 1984, 28-35; UNGERER & DAUGS 1980, 142-182; WILLIMCZIK & ROTH 1983.

2.3.2. Play Science - Play Theory - "Spiellehre"

Sport is one possible form of realizing play actions. The play element of sport can be included in different categories of games, like "new games" or games without winners, small games, partner games, large games. Forms of sport games are characterized by social interaction with each other.

Play science comprises all scientific approaches, which can contribute to the scientific explanation of the phenomenon of "play" or "games". The interdisciplinary and integrative character of this sport-specific subject field of sport science is indicated by this definition.

Play theory is a system of knowledge more or less supported by scientific research results in regard to the different meanings of play. These can be: (1) play as action realised for fun without certain aims, relaxation, enjoyment for its own sake; (2) play as action performed by a group of individuals according to certain rules in a competition, in which two teams strive to win; (3) play as a process, where events occur randomly and players play for money; (4) play as the way a player or a team is playing; (5) play as an artistic presentation; (6) in a transferred sense play means the play of waves, thoughts, forces, etc.; (7) play as a way of producing a performance easily which is normally difficult; (8) play as freedom for movement of two linked parts of a machine.

This selection of meanings of play shows, that play is a basic behaviour pattern of man with diverse meanings. Therefore, a large variety of play/game theories are available, which explain the phenomenon of play from different points of view, like philosophy, psychology, sociology, pedagogy, biology, or technology.

"Spiellehre" comprises consequently the following: systematic collection and summary of scientific knowledge on sport games and preparation of theoretical results concerning sport games for practical application. Thus "Spiellehre" involves the teaching of play like acting in sport-specific situations on the basis of the results of play/game research. Play/game theories can be differentiated according to the following positions (SCHEUERL 1975):

(a) **Phenomenological** play/game theories: here play is subordinate to a given aim; play is realised with the help of playing; this means, it depends on a certain situation and has a dynamic relation between the players and their environment (e.g., play/game theories of F.J.J. BUYTENDIJK, H. SCHEUERL, J. CHATEAU).

(b) Play/game theories on the basis of **developmental psychology and cognition**: these theories assume that there is a close connection between the development of play, the cognitive development of the individual, and the development of learning ability (e.g., play/game theories of D.B. ELKONIN, J. PIAGET).

(c) **Psychoanalytic** play/game theories: here basic motives and incentives for playing are analysed (e.g. play/game theories of E.H. ERIKSON, K. HARTMANN).

(d) **Social-psychological** play/game theories: these theories deal with role- and rule-games (e.g., play/game theories of B. KOCHAN, B. DAUBLEBSKY, S. SMILANSKY, B. SUTTON-SMITH).

The scientific knowledge constituing a play theory is especially a result of integrative and interdisciplinary sport science research.

The following **issues** are examples representing the body of knowledge of **play science-play theory = "Spiellehre"**:

Systematic analysis of play/game theories; system of sport games; socio-cultural context of sport games; rules and sport games; small games; "new games" movement; play education.

HAGEDORN (1983, 326-331) defines **play theory** as follows:

"The term playing stands for a special, voluntary form of human acting, which has mutual relationships with culture, environment, and economic conditions; in principle, it is independent of age, gender, and country; it is modified through experience. Playing is initiated by an intrinsic/extrinsic stimulus or situation; it needs a secure and known play world before it can be realised. The meaning (symbolic), process (activation), and organisation of the game are mainly determined by the way players experience themselves in dealing with reality and environment.

Play/game is the actual action context of one or more individuals; the change of tension is secured by a play/game idea and derived rules, so that the player is acting with a freedom to decide in dealing with the parameters of the play/game world. A play/game idea is the most general form of an action plan for players, from which the concrete and descriptive constitutive rules (play/game conditions) and the action-oriented regulative rules are derived.

The play/game idea as an abstract action-plan-system is rational. Every game also has its own play/game idea as independent context for action. The most general form of a play/game idea for all sport games is: motor action between two parties on an object towards two objects, which can be attacked or defended alternatively with the goal of winning".

For **further information** on **play-science-play theory** = "Spiellehre" compare the following sources: HAAG & HEIN 1990, 172-176; GRUPE & KRÜGER 1989, 208-215; GRUPE, GABLER & GÖHNER 1983; SCHEUERL 1975.

2.3.3. Training Science - Training Theory - "Trainingslehre"

Sport is an area of human acting where one can train systematically, goal-oriented, and consequently - in order to produce a sport performance - in an optimal way; it can be applied in a sport competition with the objective to be most successful. People of all ages and performance levels are willing to engage in training processes in order to reach their maximum sport performance. Therefore, engaging in sport and trainig are closly related. If the term training is used, it also includes coaching, which is part of the overall concept of training.

Training science attempts to gain knowledge about training in general and training in sport in specific. This results in many theories, which explain "training" from interdisciplinary and integrative approaches.

Training theory is a system of knowledge about the different meanings of training, gained on a more or less scientific basis. Training can be understood as planned realisation of a program of various exercises for developing ability, improving condition and coordination, as well as improving performance ability. This can be related to different behaviour dimensions of man like thinking, speaking, feeling, and moving.

"Trainingslehre" means in clear consequence the systematic collection and summary of scientific knowledge (theories) on training in sport under the aspect of organising this knowledge for practical application. Thus, "Trainingslehre" comprises training-oriented acting in sport-related situations on the basis of results of training research. One can distinguish a general "Trainingslehre" and "Trainingslehre" related to certain sport disciplines. Both forms of "Trainingslehre" are not only related to top-level athletics, but rather also have relevance for sport for all (prevention, therapy, rehabilitation).

Besides "Bewegungslehre", "Trainingslehre" is the most developed sport-specific subject field of sport science, which requires integrative and interdisciplinary procedures.

The following **issues** are examples representing the body of knowledge of **training science-training theory = "Trainingslehre"**:

training goals - training principles; content of training; training methods; training aids; analysis of prerequisites, planning, realisation, and evaluation of training in sport; training and competition; training and prevention; training and therapy; training and rehabilitation.

CARL (1983, 421) defines **"Traingslehre"** in the following way:

"A summarising and structured presentation of all goals; principles, types, contents, and methods of training, as well as a theory of competition in order to be applied in practical training. TL is developed on the basis of experience from sport practice and results of sport science research; the latter relates especially to research areas like sports medicine, performance physiology, biochemistry, biomechanics, "Bewegungslehre", sport pedagogy, (didactics, methodics), sport psychology, and sport sociology. General "Trainingslehre" deals with fundamentals valid for all sport disciplines; special "Trainingslehre" deals with the different sport disciplines and their specific sub disciplines. In the past years "Trainingslehre" has become an increasingly important and investigated issue beyond competitive sports, such as fitness sport (fitness training) as well as training for prevention and rehabilitation."

For **further information** on **training science-training theory = "Trainingslehre"** compare the following sources: CARL 1992, 223-240 (English); MARTIN 1992, 241-262 (English); HAAG & HEIN 1990, 175-190, 422; CARL 1989, 216-229; CARL 1984b, 305-328; KAYSER 1984b, 329-350; STORCK 1984, 877-916; CARL 1984a, 917-940; FREY 1984, 62-78; HILDENBRANDT 1980, 348-373.

2.3.4. Instruction Science (of Sport) - Instruction Theory (of Sport) - "Unterrichtslehre (des Sports)

Sport can be seen as sum of physical activities by which intentional or functional learning processes are realised. These many physical activities thus can serve as direct objective for teaching and learning processes (education of the body) or as vehical in order to teach and learn something through physical activities (education through the body). Taxonomies of the motor domain - like sensory abilities, conditional abilities, coordinative abilities, body experiences, sport-technical skills, and sport-tactical skills - prove the broad variability of physical activities and exercises, which can be summarized as sport and which can be used for instructional and therefore educational purposes.

Instruction science (of sport) includes all scientific approaches, which deal with teaching and learning processes, in other words instruction, in this case related to sport. Since results of several theory fields, especially sport medicine, sport biomechanics, sport psychology, and sport sociology are integrated together with results from the central relation-theory-field sport pedagogy, the interdisciplinary and integrative character of this sport-specific subject field is obvious.

Instruction theory (of sport) is besides curriculum theory (of sport) the major part of sport pedagogy as a theory field of sport science. Since instruction (and by this education) is a lifelong process and since it relates to many places, where teaching and learning takes place, the amount of instruction theories avalaible is quite large, which can guide teaching-learning processes in sport.

"Unterrichtslehre" (des Sports) means in clear consequence a systematic collection and summary of scientific knowledge (theories) on instruction in sport, under the aspect of organising this knowledge in order to be applied practically. "Unterrichtslehre" (des Sports) has close relationships to results from education as a general scientific field. It comprises what very often is understood and named as sport didactics ("Sportdidaktik") being a subtopic of sport pedagogy and dealing with questions and issues of teaching and learning processes in sport and physical activity.

The following **issues** are examples representing the body of knowledge of **instruction science (of sport) - instruction theory (of sport) = "Unterrichtslehre" (des Sports)**: Anthropological preconditions of instruction (the learner and teacher-coach); socio cultural preconditions (the social situation of the individual, the group, the institution, and the time situation); aims and objectives; content in regard to motor, cognitive, and affective domain; educational principles, methods and organisational means for teaching and learning; media and their use in instruction processes. The concepts of analysing preconditions, planning, realizing, and evaluating instruction in sport are also central issues.

Größing (1992, 426-428) defines "Unterrichtslehre" (des Sports) = "Sportdidaktik" in the following way:
"The subject matter of "Sportdidaktik" is sport instruction in schools, clubs, and other places, in which sport is used for education. It is the theory of teaching and learning in sport and is dealing with issues relevant for sport instruction and their mutual relationships; these are aims and objectives, contents, instructional methods, themes for instruction, forms for organisation and personal interaction. "Sportdidaktik" investigates and describes the aspects of planing, realizing, and evaluating teaching- and learning processes in sport; it includes conditions in regard to society, school, and personnel; it provides instructional help and action plans for the physical education teacher. As profession-related theory "Sportdidaktik" is effective, if it tries to grasp and present the complexity of instructional practice in sport".

For further information on instruction science (of sport) - instruction theory (of sport) = "Unterrichtslehre" (des Sports) compare the following sources: HAAG & HEIN 1990, 103-125, 407-410; HAAG 1989b, 48-69 - the same in English: HAAG 1992a, 329-360; PREISING 1984, 23-62; KAYSER 1984a, 63-82; GRUPE 1980b, 216-243; SCHMITZ 1980, 244-266; RIEDER & SCHMIDT 1980, 267-315.

2.4. General Subject Fields of Sport Science

In the following **seven subject fields** are presented, which are **indirectly related to movement, play, and sport.** These subject fields represent the core of sport science but also play a role in regard to other phenomena like art, music, economy etc. Like the theory fields (compare 2.1 and 2.2) and the three subject fields (compare 2.3) these seven subject fields are part of the theoretical framework for the five-volume series "Foundations for the Study of Sport Science" edited by HAAG & STRAUß (HAAG, STRAUß & HEINZE 1989; HAAG & HEIN 1990; HAAG 1991a; STRAUß & HAAG 1994).

The **seven general subject fields of sport science** are: **performance and performance ability in sport** (MECHLING 1989); **music and movement** (RÖTHIG 1989); **sport and leisure** (JÜTTING & SCHERER 1989); **sport and health** (BREHM 1989); **sport with special groups** (RIEDER & HUBER 1989); **sport and mass media** (SEIFART 1989); **aggression and violence in sport** (PILZ 1989).

The list of these general subject fields can be extended. The indicated subject fields are examples. Other proposals are: sport and administration, sport and environment, sport and age, etc. which could not be included in this analysis due to space limits.

These general subject fields of sport science are based mostly on the integration of theories and knowledge from theory fields (compare 2.1 and 2.2) and the three sport-specific subject fields (compare 2.3). Thus, the paradigm of **interdisciplinarity and integration** is applied in challenged in these subject fields. The list of general subject fields can and will be extended. In order to keep in line with certain systematic criteria and a logic approach, the level of abstraction, however, should remain similar in this possible process of extending the body of knowledge by adding further general subject fields.

The following table provides informationon these general subject fields.

The following table provides information on these general subject fields.General Subject Field	General Issue	Relation to Sport-specific Subject Fields	Relation to Theory Fields	Specific Remarks
performance and perform- ance ability in sport	performance	movement theory	sport medicine sport psychol- ogy	performance as a norm of life
music and movement	music	movement theory	sport pedagogy sport psychol- ogy	new and crea- tive movement
sport and rec- reation	leisure/rec- reation	play theory	sport pedagogy sport sociology	currently rele- vant topic
sport and health	health	training theory	sport medicine sport psychol- ogy	health is an important world-wide topic
sport with special groups	special groups	movement theory	sport psychol- ogy sport pedagogy	close connec- tion to adapted physi- cal edu- cation
sport and mass media	mass media	----	sport sociology sport psychol- ogy	relation to communication science
aggression and violence in sport	aggression and violence	----	sport sociology sport psychol- ogy	important so- cial problem

Fig. 9:   Seven-Subject-Field-Model (HAAG 1979, 1989a)

This model can be understood better, if each theme field is presented briefly with reference to the following points (HAAG 1991a, 220-271):

-- Sport under the perspective of the respective theme field.
-- Description of the theme field.
-- Examples for major content areas.
-- Definition of the theme field by a noted scholar working in the field.

2.4.1. Performance and Performance Ability in Sport

Sport is one possibility to realise performance, mainly motor-oriented (including cognitive and affective elements), on the basis of individually different perform-ance ability. Performance has to be seen as an integral part of sport and partici-pation in sport on all levels of performance. Sport, therefore, offers opportuni-ties to develop self-confidence and a feeling for self-esteem through realizing sport-related performances; thus, a positive personality development may be supported by involvement in physical activity and sport.

Performance as an integral part of sport is on one side process and on the other side product of sport actions. Performance can be measured and/or estimated. Furthermore, performance is normative, this means, performance is the optimal solution of a movement task. Performance is a very complex phenomenon due to its various predetermining factors. Consequently, **performance** is seen quite differently in the **theory fields of sport science** (compare 2.1) and thus also un-derstood in many ways in its relation to sport.

(a) **Sport medicine:** performance understood as power is the indicator for mastering a task in a time unit (kp/s or watt); aspects of performance physiology (heart, circulatory system, breathing, metabolism), but also of orthopaedics (joints, tendons, ligaments, bones) play a role in sportive per-formance.

(b) **Sport biomechanics:** performance can often be measured directly in physi-cal units of measurement.

(c) **Sport psychology:** sport performance depends on genetic components (talent) and on the specific learning processes; such motor learning proc-esses are essential for achieving a long-term change of motor behaviour.

(d) **Sport pedagogy:** sport performance is mainly seen as relative performance; this means, that performance in sport depends on factors related to the in-dividual such as degree of difficulty of the task, individual performance ability, and willingness to perform.

(e) **Sport sociology:** sport performance is viewed as depending on the following aspects: socio-cultural conditions, relations within the sport group, and norms in a society for the evaluation of sport actions.

(f) **Sport history:** from a historical point of view performance has always been connected with sport; the development of performance in sport over time has been and will be pointing upwards. However, in some sport disciplines (especially the so called cm/gr/sec sports) a levelling of the absolute performance development can be foreseen.

(g) **Sport philosophy:** from a philosophical-anthropological point of view the striving for performance is part of the basic behaviour pattern of human beings. Man, however, should decide freely to perform in sport and define his individual performance limits. Performance in sport today is often criticised; this relates to a one-sided image of top-level athletics as professional sport, in which performance is seen in an absolute way. Performance under a relative perspective can be fully accepted from a philosophical or anthropological point of view.

By defining sport performance in light of these seven existing theory fields of sport science (compare 2.1) it becomes clear, how complex and variable performance in sport is; therefore, a very differentiated judgement is necessary when dealing with performance in sport.

The following **issues** are examples representing the body of knowledge of the general subject field **"performance and performance ability in sport"** (MECHLING 1989, 230-251): the concept of performance in sport; prerequisites for the realisation of performance in sport; body constitution as prerequisite for performance; performance ability; structure of performance realisation; performance result (sport competition).

HAHN & BAUMANN (1983, 223-225) define **performance in relation to sport** in the following way:

"Performance is process and product of actions. Often also the requirements demanded of an individual, are called performance. In general, performance is the result of actions, procedures, and processes; in light of a normative interpretation performance is seen as the successful and optimal solving of a task. In social sciences the dependence of performance results is seen from given abilities and the realised processes of outside influence and learning. Beyond a sport-oriented definition of performance the following interpretations of performance can be given: Anthropological ..., cultural ..., educational ..., sociological ..., from economics ..., from physics ...".

For **further information** on **"performance and performance ability in sport"** compare the following sources: HAAG & HEIN 1990, 190-191, 424-425; MECHLING 1989, 230-251; ADL 1964.

2.4.2. Music and Movement

Sport is one form of movement, in which the relationship between music and movement can be realised very well. According to the method of performance assessment one can distinguish three types of sport disciplines: cm/g/sec sports, artistic sports, and game sports. It is obvious that the connection of music and movement can be realised best in the group of artistic sport disciplines such as rhythmical callisthenics, floor exercise in gymnastics, figure skating, roller skating, synchronised swimming, ski ballet, etc. The inclusion of music in sport acting meets the expectations of many people engaging in sport; forms like aerobics, dance, sport theatre, and callisthenics based on music have become increasingly popular. Thus, sport and music do not exclude each other, but rather have many common features.

If music and movement are related to each other, both aspects have a cooperative or mutual relationship. This can be realised in two ways:

(a) **Music** is the basis and one attempts to follow the music in movements, therefore bringing music and movement together. Movement behaviour then comprises the interpretation of music through adequate forms of movement.

(b) Certain **movement** forms are practised and one is searching for suitable music to accompany these movements.

In both cases auditive sensory input is combined with movement behaviour. The current attitude of people regards the combination of music and movement as very important; consequently, music has become more and more a part of teaching-learning processes in physical activity. From an educational point of view music and movement are seen as central aspects of education geared towards music and culture.

The following **issues** are examples representing the body of knowledge of the general subject field of sport science "**music and movement**" (RÖTHIG 1989, 252-261): music and school sport; music and sport outside of school; music and training in sport; "music and movement" in special education; "music and movement" in therapy; "music and movement" in rehabilitation.

In order to get a better understanding of the relationship of music and movement, two central terms, **rhythm and rhythmics**, are interpreted in the following by RÖTHIG (1983a, 302-303). "Rhythm is the dynamic grouping, structuring, and stressing of parts of a process, which is determined by a required and/or individually selected time scheme. The clarity of a rhythm is realised by repeating equal or similar parts. The parts of a movement process, which can be combined in rhythmic complexes, are motor skills, which can be recognised and distinguished from each other by means of their figure, space, time, and energy components. Group rhythm is a rhythmic order accepted by several individuals at the same time in equal or similar movement forms. ... In sport science the range of understanding rhythm goes from metaphysical up to biomechanical interpretations. Very often the rhythm of a movement is seen in connection with aesthetic, economic, or harmonic qualities. Thus, rhythm stands for natural, organic, true, beautiful, correct, etc. movement forms. ... Rhythmics is seen as rhythmical-musical education. Rhythmics attempts to use in rhythmical tasks the mutual relationship of movement, music, and language ... for communicative and creative ... processes in a conscious way. The learning goals of rhythmics are reached by sensory behaviour, bound to objects and situations, by using sensory qualities like hearing, seeing, touching, and moving."

For **further information** on **"music and movement"** compare the following sources: HAAG & HEIN 1990, 191-192, 425; RÖTHIG 1989, 252-261.

2.4.3. Sport and Recreation

Sport is a possible content of leisure pursuits. The origin of the word sport (from Latin "disportare" to English "to disport" = to take away, to have fun, to recreate) indicates the leisure perspective, which became relevant with the beginning of industrialisation in England at the beginning of the 19th century. Step by step sport became an important factor of social life. Today sport in connection with recreation and leisure time is becoming a more and more accepted aspect of the total social phenomenon of sport.

Recreational or leisure time sports are forms of physical activity in leisure under a time perspective. It comprises sport after work, on weekends, in vacations, in retirement, or during periods of (unfortunate) unemployment. The importance of recreational or leisure time sports is increasing constantly with the shortening of work time during the week and in the entire life. Therefore, this form of sport cannot be seen any longer only under the criteria of relaxation and rebuilding work power. Rather, it has its own value by contributing to a satisfied life. Therefore, it is characterized by aspects like self-activity, creativity, cooperation, and communication. Leisure time sport often is realised in heterogeneous groups with respect to age, gender, and performance level. Many organisations offer this type of sport: sport clubs, communities, private companies. Leisure time sport is recognised as a responsibility of educational and health politics; nevertheless it has to fight quite hard for adequate financial support. Within school sport one major aim is to educate and motivate children for the realisation of sport in leisure time. This relates to the time spent in school and outside school as well as the preparation for participating in sports throughout the entire life, especially also after school has been left.

The following **issues** are examples representing the body of knowledge of the general subject field **"sport and recreation"**: target groups and participants; socio-cultural determinants; aims and objectives; contents; methods used; recreational sports as instructional means.

DIECKERT (1983, 139-140) defines **"leisure time sport"** as follows: "Under the criterion of time leisure time sport means engaging in sport after work time and time used for daily necessities like sleeping, getting to work, eating, hygienic pursuits. In the terminology of Marx sport is realised in the time, where work energy is reproduced. The importance of sport in regard to active recreation pursuits is related to the reduction of work time ... and to the shift of life fulfilment towards recreation and away from work.

Leisure time sport is a separate form of sport in regard to goals, forms, prerequisites, realisation, results, and costs; it is to be distinguished according to its structure and content from top-level-athletics. ... Recreation, compensation, and reproduction theories have a one-sided view of this in regard to relaxation through sport; they overlook the human right of the individual for movement, play, joy, sociability and self-realisation possible in leisure time sport. In leisure time sport homogeneous groups in regard to age, gender, and performance level are possible, using contents for exercise, play, and competition bound by given rules, but also with changeable rules. ... Free methods, democratic decisions, and self-organisation enhance self-activity and creativity. Social interaction, communication, solidarity, partnership, and cooperation stand for life enrichment. Sport facilities for leisure time sport are oriented towards the needs of the users, are easy to use, have multiple applications, are variable, and have simple equipment. They have a challenging character, in other words: inviting, attracting, and exciting, they allow trials, risk, inventing, experimenting, and creative work."

For **further information** on **"sport and leisure time"** compare the following sources: HAAG & HEIN 1990, 192-194, 425-426; JÜTTING & SCHERER 1989, 262-287; KAYSER 1984b, 329-350; STEINER 1984, 535-564; HAMMERER 1984, 841-864; BÖHMER 1984a, 941-952.

2.4.4. Sport and Health

Sport has always been seen in connection with health. On the one hand, one can assume, that sport and physical activity enhance health in different dimensions, depending on how sport is realised. On the other hand one also has to recognise that certain forms of engagement in sport are detrimental to ones health, e.g. when injuries and illnesses are provoked as a result of engaging in sport. Therefore, the relation between sport and health has to be seen in an ambivalent way; however, the positive perspective generally prevails over negative aspects of sport.

Health sport is every kind of sport action, in which it is central to regain, maintain, or improve one's health status. From a medical point of view health sport is an important instrument for prevention, therapy, and rehabilitation. Four aspects of human behaviour are explained with negative examples.

(a) Physical aspects: lack of movement, wrong nutrition, stress, smoking.

(b) Mental aspects: lack of attention, reduced reaction ability, low cognitive alertness, and lack of flexibility.

(c) Psychological aspects: emotions like depression, fatigue, self-doubts, aggression.

(d) Social aspects: lack of social skill, problems in social interaction, egocentricism, unfairness towards others.

In order to cope with such deficits, in other words to regain, maintain, or to improve health in a holistic way, certain forms of health education are used; one such form is health training. They represent educational actions in order to transmit knowledge, attitudes, and ways of acting to leading to a health-conscious way of life in all situations; movement, play, and sport are important for realizing this aim.

The following **issues** are examples representing the body of knowledge of the general subject field **"sport and health"**: From the point of view of an individual; under an integrative point of view; in top-level athletics; in state educational institutions; in sport clubs; within commercial settings for practising sport.

In order to understand health sport as a general subject field of sport science it seems reasonable to give a definition of the terms **health education** (BERNETT 1983, 150-151) and **health training** (KAYSER 1983, 150-151), since they relate to physical activity and sport.

"Health education is in principle a task for all educators to counteract the psycho-physical stress in schools, to call for an understandable idea of health, to enhance a healthy way of life, and to transmit relevant knowledge. Health education is necessary due to the requirement of a healthy routine during the school day. The counselling of children by school doctors with health problems is part of the responsibility of the school towards better health. Health education includes: life attitudes, abuse of drugs, nutrition, body hygiene, movement challenge through sport, and - according to the definition of health by the WHO - also aspects of social well-being. In a broader sense health education is also

Since it is not possible within the scope of this work to define all possible special groups, three examples are given: **"sport for adults over 40"** (SINGER & UNGERER-RÖHRICH 1983, 22-23), **"sport for children with coordination problems"** (RÖTHIG 1983b, 136), **"sport for handicapped"** (HAAG 1987, 72-73), **"sport in prison"** (KOFLER 1983, 145), .

"The term sport for adults over 40 (age differentiation) stands for sport for people beyond 40 years, but also the group after retirement (60/65 years of age), called sport for seniors, ... starting with about 50 the regression and devolution phenomena of different kinds can be seen gradually, and are registered clinically, and have to be considered in the planning of sport involvement. ... Health aspects are considered predominantly in choosing contents and methods for sport for adults over 40. ... Other important aims have to remain in the background, e.g., social-communicative acting with the aim of integrating people, enjoyment and contentment, as well as self-activity".

"Sport for children with coordinations problems (performance differentiation) is a supplementary program offered within school physical education. It is aimed towards children and young people, who have deficiencies in their motor performance ability due to psycho-physical weakness. ... By help of individual programs learning deficiencies caused, e.g., by sickness, accidents etc., may be compensated".

Sport for Handicapped ("Behindertensport") comprises all forms of physical activity practised by handicapped people with the aim of movement therapy, sport for recreation or competitive sport (e.g. Paralympics). The physical exercises and sport disciplines are adapted to the different handicaps of the people engaging in physical activities. For the competitive level different classes are defined in order to provide fair chances for the participants having different disabilities. This also applies to the top level of athletics like the Paralympics. On the school level there are different types of schools for handicapped people. The movement education and physical activity is of special importance in the educational process for the people with different handicaps.

"Sport in prison (social differentiation) is sport realised in prison institutions. Since the organisational frame is mostly characterized by security and order, there is a conflict in regard to the free room which is needed by sport. ... So far sport in prison has been seen primarily under compensatory aspects (working against lack of movement and compensation for the monotony in prison). ... In light of a holistic view of the prisoners, research on sport in prison must, however, consider pedagogical, sport-pedagogical, deep-psychology-oriented, as well as sociological aspects; it is necessary to keep close contact with the reality prison".

related to the building aspects of a school. ... The application of the term health training requires that health is seen as a construct, which can be measured and improved in regard to the functional condition of organs and organ-systems; it is necessary to define health in this context as a parameter, which can be defined on scales and neither as "complete physical, mental, and social well-being" (WHO), nor as "freedom of sickness" in a classical sense. The main points of health training are prevention against risk factors connected with lack of movement and retardation of the ageing process."

For **further information** on **"sport and health"** compare the following sources: HAAG & HEIN 1990, 194-196, 427-428; BREHM 1989, 288-301; NITSCH & CHRISTEN 1984, 565-586; RITTNER 1984, 607-620; DORDEL 1984 773-792; BÖHMER 1984, 941-952.

2.4.5. Sport with Special Groups

Sport offers the opportunity to provide programs for active participation of special groups in sport. While prevention through sport is related to the normal situation of people, therapy and rehabilitation in regard to sport offer possibilities for participation of special groups in sport. Thus, sport for handicapped has become an important part of the sport system.

Movement, play, and sport are seen as forms of action, which can be realised by all people. Besides the majority of people, who have developed "normally" and who lead a normal life, there are many special groups, which often are on the edge of the society. The so-called social force of sport or the social political possibilities of movement, play, and sport can and must reach especially these people. A society has a responsibility towards the highly talented people, e.g. in top-level athletics, but also towards these special groups.

Out of the four questions "why, who, where, when" of engaging in sport, under the perspective of **"sport with special groups"** the question "who" could be answered in the following way: sport for seniors, sport for handicapped, sport in kindergarten, sport for unemployed people, sport with immigrants, sport with groups with certain kinds of illness, and sport with socially deprived groups (e.g., drugs, alcohol, prison). Sport with special groups is an area, in which the social-political responsibility of the world of sport meets a big challenge.

The following **issues** are examples representing the body of knowledge of the general subject field of **"sport with special groups"**: sport programs according to age-differentiation; sport programs according to performance differentiation; sport programs according to ability differentiation; sport programs according to social differentiation.

For **further information** on "sport with special groups" compare the following sources: HAAG & HEIN 1990, 197-199, 428-430; RIEDER & HUBER 1989, 302-315; DORDEL 1984, 773-792.

2.4.6. Sport and Mass Media

Sport has become a major content of the different mass media. Sport as spectator sport, as passive sport, has received a high status within possible leisure activities, besides sport as physically active participation. So far there is a direct and very intensive connection with mass media, which have a high - often not recognised - responsibility for the development of sport as a social phenomenon.

Sport journalism is related to all mass media, which participate in the public information and judgement process concerning sport. **Mass media** are:

(a) Sport newspapers (sport section of "general" newspapers): they are published periodically, usually daily, report on all aspects of sport, and comment on single aspects or events.

(b) Sport journals: they are published less frequently. Two forms can be distinguished: journals for sport theory or sport disciplines and sport magazines of a more popular character. These journals are published either by publishing companies or by sport associations.

(c) Sport TV: verbal and visual information on sport in reports, comments, and interviews (also exclusive sport channels).

(d) Sport film: the following categories can be distinguished: TV films with sport elements; sport films with elements of a TV film; documentary films; teaching and instruction films; sport scientific films.

(e) Sport radio: verbal information on sport in reports, comments, and interviews.

(f) Sport photography: pictures of sport movements, also as part of other visual media on posters, in calendars, in books etc.

The most important task of sport journalism is to report on current sport events; however, it also has a responsibility to reflect on the connection of sport and politics, education, culture, and economy.

The term **sport journalistics** stands for research and teaching in regard to communication via media in sport. Important tasks are investigations of the following; connection between receiver and emitter; structure of the audience; social-psychological effects of sport-oriented media for communication, sport terminology and language, as well as training of sport journalists.

The following **issues** are examples representing the body of knowledge of the general subject field **"sport and mass media"**: forms of transmission of sport-oriented mass media; the relationship between emitter and receiver of reports on sport; sport-oriented mass media and sport language; sport-oriented mass media in the information society.

KREBS (1983, 355-356) defines **sport journalistics** ("Sportpublizistik") in the following way:

"Sport journalistics is the application of knowledge and methods of journalisitcs as the science of mass communication to the specific communication process, where reports are given on events from the world of sports. Generally speaking sport journalistics is the reporting on sport events in the mass media (press, radio, tv, film) and as such equal to sport journalism. Sport journalistics is part of communication science, which deals with communication in general, and deals analogously with the following topics, using mainly methods of social science: issues of the communicator (sport journalist, sport editor, team for making films, videos, pictures) content analysis of the output of the communicators, principles for making media, general issues, and their conditions, the antithesis of action and presentation performance (Gebauer). ... Quality of mass media for the respective audience, and feedback from the public audience to the communicator. Sport journalistics analyses the historical and sociological dimensions of sport journalism; it attempts to create a critical understanding of the practice of journalists; finally, the journalists receive empirical research results and ideas regarding the function of sport journalists and regarding the fact, that the content of mass media has social-psychological effects."

For **further information** on **"sport and mass media"** compare the following sources: HAAG & HEIN 1990, 199-201, 430-431; SEIFART 1989, 316-325; KIRSCH 1984, 757-772.

2.4.7. Aggression and Violence in Sport

Sport is a main public phenomenon, it can be connected with positive (e.g., fun, happiness), but also with negative (e.g., aggression, violence) aspects. These negative developments have the consequence, that tendencies to pervert sport, which also have an impact on sport as a cultural factor, have to be observed attentively. This is especially important, since otherwise the danger exists that the positive possibilities and values inherent in movement, play, and sport are distorted. Sport does resemble tendencies of perversion, such as aggression/violence, doping, top-level athletics with children; sport is connected with the developments in society as a whole.

The terms used in this general subject field **"aggression and violence in sport"** seem to be contradictory to sport, since usually terms like fairness, cooperation etc. are connected with sport. However, sport - just like other cultural sectors - is open for tendencies like ideology, commercialisation, professionalisation, bureaucratisation and perversion.

The ethical-normative responsibility of sport can be seen threefold: towards oneself, towards others, and towards the environment/nature. Aggressive/violent actions are possible in all three directions. Doping is a kind of violence towards oneself, against the nature of man; unfair behaviour, maybe with physical injuries as a consequence, is aggression/violence against others; unconscious and unreflected dealing with nature - in doing sports like skiing in areas where it is not permitted - is something like aggression/violence against nature and the environment.

This threefold relation of aggression/violence to sport indicates that it is an important current issue and that one has to deal with this problem. This relates to the analysis of the origin of aggression/violence up to the search for means to cope with aggression/violence; this can be done under a short-term (police in sport arenas), middle-term (support of fan projects) and long-term (education to and through sport on an ethical-normative basis) perspective.

The following **issues** are examples representing the body of knowledge of the general subject field **"aggression and violence in sport"**: analysis of the preconditions of aggression and violence in sport; aggression and violence of athletes; aggression and violence of spectators; means to limit aggression and violence in sport.

STÜTZLE (1983, 17) describes the topic of **aggression in sport** as follows:

"Aggression research related to sport investigates the relationship between sport and aggression. This is done mainly in studies (with contradicting results) on the aggressiveness of athletes of different sport disciplines and by comparisons with individuals who do not engage in sport. Furthermore, it is examined, whether the participation in competitions, the possibilities to show aggressive behaviour within a game, or the physical exhaustion of the athletes have cathartic effects; the same is investigated for the spectator, if there are effects of catharsis through the emotional engagement of the spectator in the event, the quasi (for the spectator) aggression of the athlete or the quasi (for the spectator) exhaustion of the athlete."

Within the **"Magglingen Theses"** (HAAG, KIRSCH & KINDERMANN 1991, 107) **violence** is characterized by **five theses**:

"Thesis 1: In regard to top-level athletics the increasing violance is criticised frequently today. As it stands, physical violence with the aim to hurt the opponent without direct performance aims has diminuished in top-level athletics. At the same time, however, aggressions with the aim to make performance advantages, have increased. This development is also due to professionalisation and commercialisation.

Thesis 2: Violance as physical contest can be a sport discipline-specific structural sign and therefore conform with the rules. However, sport ceases to be ethical, where by not coping with sport discipline-specific rules and norms aggression, brutality, and cheating prevail.

Thesis 3: A central problem of competitive sport is the increase of aggressions with the aim to win at any rate. This may result in norms being changed towards unfair, physical, and verbal contests.

Thesis 4: Aggressions of spectators can be influenced by the sport event; they are, however, first of all a social problem, especially of young people.

Thesis 5: Athletes and officials have to create and nurture the sport which matches their expectations. In order to guide sport in the expected direction, an early and comprehensive education towards fair play is necessary."

For **further information** on **"aggression and violence in sport"** compare the following sources: HAAG & HEIN 1990, 202, 431-432; PILZ 1989, 326-344; PILZ 1982.

Conclusion

The **body of knowledge** or **content dimension** of every scientific discipline is a very fundamental question and therefore a major issue of the respective scientific theory or meta-theory. There are different ways of presenting the content of sport science in a logically structured way. GRUPE (1971, 7-18),e.g., proposes to categorise the content according to the framework where sport is realised: youth sport, school physical education, competitive sport, and top-level athletics. Similar and comparable structural models of the reality of sport are described in chapter 4.1, 4.2, and 4.3, where the necessary transfer of research results to the practice of sport is discussed.

Within this analysis, however, it was decided to use the **disciplinary-oriented theory-field approach** and the **theme-oriented subject-field approach**. The latter one is close to different units of the reality of sport.

It also has to be made clear, that with this **dual approach** of theory-field and subject field, of discipline and theme, of science and topic, of specific and integrated, a comprehensive perception of the content of sport science is possible. Several points have to be considered in regard to the **dimension of content/body of knowledge of a science** like sport science:

(a) **Sport** science is a **young science** and therefore the construct of content has to be further developed.

(b) **Sport** is a constantly **increasing** and **differentiating phenomenon** with consequences for its scientific treatment.

(c) The **range of possible contents** is very **large**, e.g., from sport medicine to sport philosophy, from recreation to health, from sport-for-all to top-level athletics.

(d) The content always has to be seen on a comparable level of abstraction, if strategies of a **hierarchic structure** of a **thesaurus** are used for content description.

(e) Movement, play, and sport are **international** by nature. This also has consequences for the content, since it should have a certain degree of multicultural character.

Despite the difficulty in dealing with these five points, there is a lot of positive and constructive potential to guide the development of sport science in an appropriate direction. The **structural model for the content of sport science** (two groups of **theory fields** and two groups of **subject fields**) or the presentation of its body of knowledge in this analysis is one way of giving an answer on the important question regarding the content-dimension of the scientific theory or meta-theory of sport science.

3. Research Methodology in Sport Science.
Or: What is the Process of Gaining Scient.. Knowledge in Sport Science?

Introduction

Aspects related to the ways and conditions of gaining knowledge in a scientific manner ultimately decide on the academic status of a certain scientific discipline. This is again a specific challenge to a relatively young discipline like sport science. On the one hand, this academic discipline has to follow the different developments in **research methodology** carefully **on a general level** (BORTZ 1984; KERLINGER 1986; KEEVES 1988; KRIZ & LISCH 1988). On the other hand, it is necessary to develop **own strategies and techniques** for carrying out the research process **within sport science**. In the beginning of the development of a scientific field aspects of research methodology of the "mother" or related science are often applied in the emerging scientific field. Step by step, however, it is necessary to also develop research methodology from the point of view of the new scientific discipline, in this case of sport science.

Within this context a model for research methodology in sport science has been developed, the so-called **"Kiel Model of Research Methodology"** (KMRM), which distinguishes **six different steps**, representing a sequence of aspects that constitute the logic order of the research process (HAAG 1991b, 291-306; HAGER & WESTERMANN 1983; HAGER 1987).

Within an introductory phase of the research process basic questions related to the **philosophy of science** ("Wissenschaftsphilosophie") are asked; it is at this stage that research problems originate. Especially aspects of **epistemology** ("Erkenntnistheorie") and aspects of **scientific theory (different positions)**

Wissenschaftstheoretische Positionen") (compare TOULMIN 1981; SEIFERT & RADNITZKY 1989) are taken into consideration.

During the historical development of science in general, different prominent positions in regard to the **philosophy of science** have been developed. Within the research process it is absolutely necessary that the researcher, this means the individuals involved in research, has a scientific position which provides a theoretical framework for the research process to be followed.

After considering basic aspects of scientific theory the fundamental question has to be dealt with, namely, which **research methods** should be applied. This means, a discussion of various research concepts as indicated in antithetical terms like rationalistic-naturalistic, experimental-descriptive, empirical/analytical-hermeneutical/theoretical. It is necessary for every research process, that a decision is made in regard to the dimension of research methods depending on the given research theme.

On a next more concrete level **research designs** have to be considered (BORTZ 1984), which best fit the research topic, for which hypotheses or basic assumptions have been formulated. Within the research design many detailed aspects of the research process have to be followed diligently. If the planning work for a research process has been carefully realised at this level by considering these relevant aspects, it is likely, that the research process will be followed in a correct and effective way.

Data collection is the next step within this research process (BRICKENKAMP 1975, 1983, 1986; BORTZ 1984; JÄGER 1988). The data base and its delimitation (sampling) as well as the respective techniques of data collection are of utmost importance. At this stage of the research process sport-specific aspects become more and more important, since the situation in which data are collected is in most cases a sport-specific one. Thus, the quality of data collection techniques decides to a great extent on the quality of the research produced.

The next logic step following the collection of data is **data analysis**; techniques are required for two typical cases: hermeneutical strategies for data coded in words; statistical strategies for data coded in numbers. Both avenues for data analysis are necessary. The latter one has been successfully developed in many statistical concepts; the former so-called hermeneutical strategies, still require more detailed development.

The last step in this logic sequence of research methodology is the important aspect of applying the research results to the practical situation through **knowledge transfer**. At present there are many deficiencies in this transfer dimension. Several basic aspects of a scientific theory which are relevant in the first step of the KMRM have to be considered again in this last step of a logically followed research process.

Fig. 10 illustrates the " Logic Research Sequence" which is the basis of the KMRM (HAAG) in more detail .

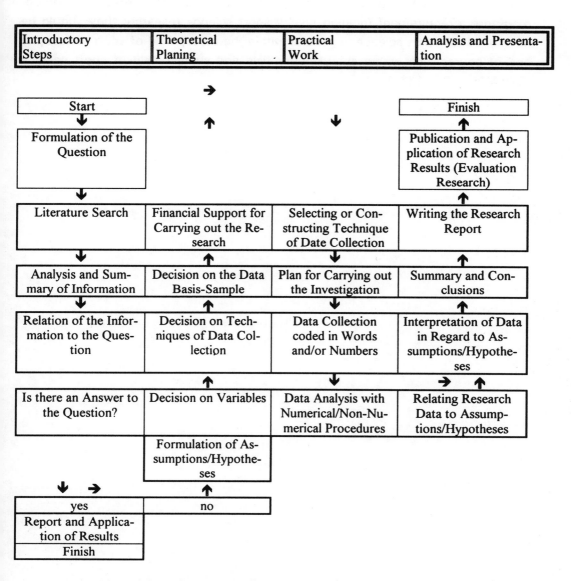

Fig. 10: Logic Research Sequence (HAAG)

In summary, the question **"What is the process of gaining scientific knowledge in sport science?"** has to be answered in a very differentiated manner. The six-step KMRM is a possible solution to this request. There might be other concepts of research methodology. It is important, however, that research methodology in sport science is seen as a major aspect of the theoretical foundation of sport science as a scientific discipline. Thus, satisfactory models of research methodology are a requirement for high quality sport science research; they should be developed for sport science in general within the theory field of sport philosophy and of course also within every theory field and subject field of sport science (STRAUß 1991, 433-453).

3.1. Initial Phase of the Research Process (Philosophy of Science)

At the beginning of every research process, aspects of philosophy of science **(epistemology and scientific theory-different positions)** have to be considered (SEIFFERT 1983-1985). Within general scientific theory, as a sub discipline of philosophy, certain "schools" or positions have been developed; examples are: CARNAP 1959 - logical empirism; FEYERABEND 1976 - anarchic epistemology; HABERMAS 1968 - critical theory; HÜBNER 1978 - historism; LORENZON & SCHWEMMER 1975 - constructivism; KUHN 1967 - theory of change in paradigms; POPPER 1935 - critical rationalism; SNEED 1971 - structuralism. Independent of these models everyone engaging in research has to deal with aspects of the philosophy of science on an individual basis (SEIFFERT & RADNITZKY 1989; CHALMERS 1986).

In regard to **epistemology**, i.e., the issues of ultimate interest and importance, namely how knowledge can be gained scientifically, three positions can be distinguished on a continuum: hermeneutics is the one pole, empiricism the other pole, and phenomenology is in the middle of this continuum. A short explanation of the three positions is given in the following:

Hermeneutical means that one can gain knowledge on the basis of understanding and interpreting available material, mostly texts and documents (example: UNESCO-International Charta for Physical Education and Sport (1978/1982) or objects like the ski museum in Oslo). This is done either informally or by following formal procedures such as content analysis.

Empirical means, that on the basis of the sensory ability of seeing (partly also hearing) a clear observation can be made; these observations are exact and can be tested in their perception by other individuals (degree of inter-subjective examination) (example: measuring a long jump or stopping a time) (HIRTZ 1987, 63-88).

Phenomenological means, that one is perceiving something empirically and at the same time one attempts to understand and interpret it hermeneutically (example: perceiving a movement and interpreting it as a coach does when giving corrections or as movement in pantomime).

Phenomenological is on the continuum of hermeneutical and empirical somewhat in the middle; it is a reconciliation of seeing and understanding, since both aspects play a role in phenomenology. The phenomenological approach is used quite often in daily life. It is, however, also one unique approach to gaining scientific knowledge, besides hermeneutical and empirical as two separate approaches.

The following figure indicates, how these tracks of epistemology are related to basic contents of sport science expressed in the seven-theory-field model (compare 2.1) (HAAG 1979; HAAG 1991a).

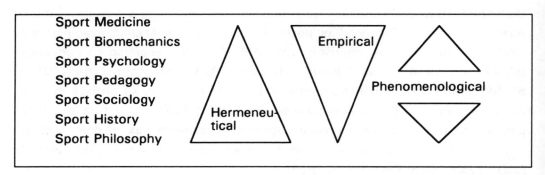

Fig. 11: Relation between Theory Fields of Sport Science and Epistemological Positions (HAAG 1991b, 295)

It is becoming clear, that there is not a better or worse, a more valuable or not so valuable way to gain knowledge. A plurality in scientific approaches is necessary; the issue to be investigated decides on how knowledge in regard to these issues is gained scientifically.

The second aspect of the philosophy of science, namely the scientific theory positions, will be analysed in light of three dimensions of the research process, which are also valid for sport science research (FRIEDRICHS 1976).

a) Discovering the research question
This first dimension of the research process is related to the justification of the research to be undertaken. The initiation and promotion of a research process can be done from **three starting points:**
Firstly, research projects can be initiated by organisations or institutions, which are interested in the scientific investigation of certain topics or issues. This so-called "Auftragsforschung" (**contract research**) is often questioned, since it is sometimes difficult for the researcher to remain independent, a requirement that is necessary in scientific endeavour. If criteria of scientific ethics are met, however, this kind of initiation of research is acceptable (NITSCH 1989; WILLIMCZIK 1989).

Secondly, research projects originate by **observation of problems,** open questions, or current topics through the researcher him-/herself. If this is done in close connection with the relevant practical field (compare chapter 4), an ideal situation for generating hypotheses or assumptions for sport science research is given.

Thirdly, research projects are started on the basis of **doubts** about whether **existing theories** explain reality correctly. Theories are re-examined in such research projects. This also relates to the different range of acceptability of a theory (short, middle, long range) in regard to whether it is scientifically proven or not.

(b) Realizing the research project

This second dimension of the research process is related to the different steps in carrying out the research project with the aim of gaining scientifically acceptable result. This includes step 2 to 5 of the **"Kiel Model of Research Methodology"** (KMRM); they are explained in more detail below in this chapter (3.2 research methods; 3.3 research designs; 3.4 techniques of data collection; 3.5 techniques of data analysis). In this dimension of the research process it can be seen often, that one-sided dogmatic positions are realised in perpetuating either a hermeneutical-theoretical or an empirical-analytical research approach. However, taking such dogmatic points of view is in contradiction with scientific criteria.

(c) Applying the research results

The third dimension of the research process is related to application of research results after the end of the research project. This aspect is described in more detail within step 6 ("Concluding Phase of the Research Process (Knowledge Transfer") of the KMRM, which is also the main topic of chapter 4 ("Transfer of Knowledge in Sport Science. Or: What is the Practice-Theory and Theory-Practice Paradigm?"). It should be mentioned briefly at this point, that the way research results are applied is a clear distinctive criterion for an evaluation of the different positions of scientific theory.

This last consideration is also the reason, why the three phases of the research process (discovering, realizing, applying) are mentioned in this context. The different positions of scientific theory have each a more or less different perceptions of the function and realisation of these three phases.

In the following figure **six examples of positions of scientific theory** are included with their relation to discovery, realisation, and application of sport science research. Some basic characteristics of the six positions are given in a separate column in order to make the positions of scientific theory more understandable.

Positions of Scientific Theory	Discovering Context Recognition	Realizing Hermeneutical Approach	Realizing Empirical Approach	Applying Context Recognition	Basic Remarks
1. Subjective Idealism (PLATON)	0	+	-	0	Individually oriented; science for the science sake
2. Dialectic Materialism (FETSCHER 1983)	+	0	0	+	Science serving the DIAMAT in order to prove its superiority; society oriented
3. Critical Theory (HABERMAS 1975)	+	+	0	+	Position bound to social necessities
4. Critical Rationalism (POPPER 1935)	0	-	+	-	Position accepting knowledge, as long as it is not falsified
5. Logical Empirism (KRAFT 1968)	0	-	+	0	Connection of cognitive and empirical dimensions in scientific work
6. Positivism (SCHNÄDEL-BACH 1989)	-	-	+	-	Empirical foundation, but little attention to considerations before or after realizing research

Tab. 3:   Positions of Scientific Theory in Regard to Discovering, Realizing, and Applying Sport Science Research (HAAG 1991b, 298) (+ strong, 0 neither/nor, - weak)

The content of this figure shows, that the specific character of different positions of scientific theory can be made clear in relating the different theoretical positions to the three phases of research (discovering, realizing, and applying).

In this first step of the KMRM it can be seen, that dealing with aspects of the philosophy of science (epistemology and/or scientific theory) is a day to day challenge within every research process and not only an abstract field for philosophical discussions. In regard to scientific theory in sport science GRUPE (1971), HAAG (1979, 1983, 1991b), LIEBER (1988), MEINBERG (1984), and WILLIMCZIK (1968, 1979) etc. have provided thoughts for discussion.

3.2. Research Methods

The second step in the KMRM has to be seen within the logic research process as the starting point for the concrete realizing phase of sport science research. The relevant question is, which basic research concepts or research methods should be used in order to deal with a concrete topic. It is important to note at this point, that the topic, issue, or question for research decides on the direction of research methods (HAAG 1991b, 46-67; ZIMMER & KLIMPEL 1987, 11-48; SCHNABEL 1987, 49-62).

Two examples of possible research projects can introduce the two **concepts for research methods**, which are described in more detail later.

1. Topic for a sport science research project: "What is the fitness level of students starting school in Bavaria?" This implies the systematic description of the fitness level, which then allows for certain consequences to be taken.

2. Topic for a sport science research project: "Which swimming technique (breast or crawl) is more useful for teaching non-swimmers how to swim?" Two samples have to be selected and given different forms of instruction (breast and crawl) in order to get an answer to the research question; afterwards the suitable swimming technique can be used in swimming instruction for beginners.

From an analysis of general and sport science specific literature for research methodology (STRAUß 1990; HUBBARD 1973; CLARKE & CLARKE 1970; THOMAS & NELSON 1990) it becomes obvious, that two basic research methods can be distinguished, **description and experiment** (other models are: qualitative-quantitative (HAAG 1991, 69-76); naturalistic-realistic (GUBA & LINCOLN 1988, 81-85)). Both can be regarded as two poles of a continuum of research methods standing for variations of research methods on the basis of the two poles. This implies a more narrow use of the term method, which is not common in sport science literature (see the "philosophic method" - MORLAND 1973).

(a) Description as a research method concept

Description is a research method for gaining knowledge in regard to given situations. No manipulation or changing of the situation to be investigated occurs. The description can be related to **different time** (historical or status quo) and **space** (different units; e.g., states) **dimensions**. If data gained in a situation analysis are compared in a **vertical** (historical) or **horizontal** (geographic units) line, correlative investigations are given; thus correlations are established (equalities, inequalities, similarities), without explaining directly why it is as it is; this latter endeavour can be pursued in an experiment. Description can also serve as a method for comparative research perspectives in sport science (compare example one for a research topic above).

(b) Experiment as a research method concept

Experiment is a research method, for gaining knowledge from situations, where intentional changes have been realised by means of intervention in order to investigate about cause-effect-relations. This specific characteristic of the experiment as a research method, namely change of independent variables (manipulation in a positive sense), has to be controlled in order to exclude intervening and distorting effects; thus, it is possible to make statements on cause-effect results (compare example two for a research project above) (CAMPBELL & STANLEY 1963; BORTZ 1984, 363-523; HUBER 1987; SARRIS 1990a,b; PHILIPP 1987, 89-119).

Both concepts of a research method are explained in some more detail in step three of the KMRM, "Research Designs". These designs can be grouped according to the basic concept description and experiment, always bearing in mind, that the **continuum paradigm** has to be seen also in this context with the **two poles description** and **experiment**.

In regard to the two concepts for research methods (description and experiment) it has to be pointed out, that for both research approaches **empirical-analytical and hermeneutical-theoretical** (and consequently also phenomenological) ways to gain knowledge are acceptable. This is important, since all too often the characteristic "empirical-analytical" is used incorrectly as being interchangeable with experimental. Within **description** and **experiment data can be coded in words and/or numbers**.

The presented model for research methodology (KMRM) can be regarded as a well-balanced model; it does not accept the sometimes hostile separation into hermeneutical-theoretical and empirical-analytical research approaches, which can be seen in the historical development of science all too often. Especially sport science depends on an open position in this regard, as expressed in the continuum paradigm. Only within such an **open concept of research methodology** is it possible to deal with a large range of questions in sport science (from sport medicine to sport philosophy) in a scientifically responsible way. It its also important to discuss future developments in regard to new research methods such as, for example, the modelling method (GUTEWORT & THORAUER 1987, 121-150).

3.3. Research Designs

The third step in the KMRM has to be seen - as mentioned - in close relation to step two "research methods". The characterisation of the realizing phase of a research process by only two basic research methods (description and experiment) would be too vague and theoretical. Concrete procedures for both research methods, namely research designs, can be developed, which describe the logic research process in more detail. In this context specific characteristics of different procedures in the process of gaining scientific knowledge in sport play an important role. Step one and two as well as step five and six of the KMRM have a relatively general scientific character; step three ("research design") and step four ("techniques of data collection"), however, are influenced more strongly by sportspecific aspects besides the basic general scientific character.

The following **issues** have to be considered in developing **research designs** (examples for sport science research) (HAAG 1991b, 300-301).

a) **Number of considered variables** (mono-, bi-, multivariable research designs). Example: monovariate → fitness, bivariate → fitness and motivation; multivariate → fitness, motivation, member of a sport club, socio-economic status.

b) **Standardisation of the research situation** (problem of intervening variables). Example: attitude towards sport, health status, personal problems.

c) **Time-dimension of the investigation** (cross-sectional, longitudinal). Example: cross-sectional → fitness of school children (grade 1) in all large cities (beyond 500.000) in Germany; longitudinal → fitness of physical education students at the beginning of the study of sport science, after two years, and after the examination.

d) **Selecting the sample from a given population** (single-case study (SCHLICHT 1988; PETERMANN 1989) or representative study (ERDMANN 1988). Example: single-case study → task, structure, and performance of the German Olympic Institute Berlin; representative study → state of fitness of primary school children in Bavaria).

e) **Number of employed techniques of data collection** (1-n techniques; triangulation by using more than one technique of data collection - compare step 4 of the KMRM). Example: content analysis of the "Charta of German Sports" (1960); physical fitness: HARO Fitness-Test, and diagnosis with medical parameters.

f) **Coding of data (words and/or numbers).** Example: word → the writings of F. L. Jahn concerning the "Deutsches Turnen"; number → long jump distance; (compare step 5 of the KMRM.

g) **Techniques of data analysis** (non-numerical-hermeneutical/numerical-statistical). Example: hermeneutical → interpretation, concluding; statistical → mean, standard deviation; compare step 5 of the KMRM.

h) **Ideas for application of research results** (compare step 6 of the KMRM and chapter 4). Example → lecture, publication in a journal).

Since step three "research designs" is relatively concrete, there are consequently many **examples for research designs.** The following figure contains some of these examples, distinguished according to the two concepts for research methods: description and experiment (LINDQUIST 1953; WINER 1971; KEPPEL 1982; KIRK 1982).

	Research Methods	
Description Concept		**Experimental Concept**
	Examples of Research Designs	
Historical (before 1900)	**Experiment with one group**	
Contemporary historical (after 1900)	(Quasi experimant)	
Ethnographic (including sociocultural enviroment)	**Experiment with two groups** (Classic control group design)	
Action-research (holistic and interactive approach)	**Experiment with more than two groups** (possibility of control for further variables)	
Cross-cultural comparison (at least two different cultural units)		

Fig. 12:   Structural Model for Research Methods / Research Designs (HAAG 1991b, 301)

It pays off to work very diligently at this level of research design, since this allows for a clear plan for the investigation, thus minimising possible mistakes or problems in the research process.

3.4. Techniques of Data Collection

Like step three step four is also linked very closely to sport science research. Techniques of data collection have been discussed within sport science only to a small extent. Techniques of data collection from the "mother" or related science of sport science theory fields (e.g., psychology (BRICKENKAMP 1975, 1983, 1986)) were often used, even if they were not developed for sport-specific situations. Therefore, the data collection frequently contained errors which could not be corrected later in the research process.

Recently, sport science has put more effort into **developing techniques** of data collection that are adequate **for sport-specific data-collection situations**. This can be described as so-called fundamental research, which in a longer perspective has application relevance and therefore is applied research in a broader sense. This is an indication that the sharp distinction between **fundamental and applied research** (often accompanied by hostile exclusive arguments) is not very reasonable (DOSE 1991, 282-291).

The increased development of techniques of data collection relates especially to the motor domain, but also to affective and cognitive behaviour dimensions in their relation to sport. Status and quality of sport science research depends to a great extent on the availability of techniques of data collection developed under observation of test theoretical criteria. If no technique of data collection is available for a certain research topic, it is necessary to developed such a technique by following the known standardised (sometimes time-consuming) procedure. There are, however, publications available on techniques of data collection: Germany: BÖS 1987; FETZ & KORNEXL 1993; GROSSER & STARISCHKA 1981; HAAG & DASSEL 1981; KRÜGER & NIEDLICH 1985; RAPP & SCHODER 1977; SINGER & WILLIMCZIK 1985; WILLIMCZIK 1983; English speaking countries: BARROW, McGEE & TRITSCHLER 1989; KIRKENDALL & GRUBER 1987 DARST, ZAKRAJSEK & MANCINI 1989; SAFRIT 1990).

There are **three main possibilities for categorising techniques of data collection**: according to the **theory fields** of sport science (e.g., sports medicine), according to **subject fields** of sport science (e.g., movement theory), and according to **formal criteria**. The last possibility will be used in the following description of techniques of data collection (SCHNABEL, GUTEWORT, HIRTZ & KLIMPEL 1987, 181-230).

(a) Content analysis: This means to analyse, understand, and interpret texts with the help of a category-system. The development of a good category-system is most important for getting the relevant data. Content analysis can, however, also be applied to objects (pictures, equipment, etc.) and actions. The data gained from a content analysis are mostly coded in words. However, numbers are also possible (ZIMMER & KLIMPEL 1987, 151-180).

Examples for data coded in words **are**: Colymbetes' "Book on Swimming"; Jahn's "German Turnen"; Gaulhofer-Streicher's "Natural Turnen"; the German Sport Federation's "Charta of the German Sport" (1960); the German Sport Federation's "Basic Declaration Regarding Top-Level Athletics" (1987). Quantitative strategies also can be used.

(b) Observation (FAßNACHT 1979; HASEMANN 1983; LAMNECK 1988, 1989): It is based on registration of motor and affective behaviour with categories, which describe the relevant construct as realistic as possible. The quality of categories again is very important. One distinguishes between self- and external observation, participatory and non-participatory forms of observation. The results of an observation are coded in words and/or numbers.

Examples are: Skills in sport disciplines like long jump (cm - gr - sec - sport discipline), somersault in gymnastics (artistic sport discipline), jump-shot in basketball (game sport discipline); technical-tactical skill in games (e.g., looking for free space); cooperation in sport games (social-affective components); anxiety in extreme sport-specific situations (individual-affective components); behaviour of physical education teachers/coaches in sport instruction/training.

(c) Interview (MUMMENDAY 1987): Directed towards affective and cognitive aspects of sport as well as sport-specific actions. Interviews can be realised by formal **(questionnaire)** or more informal (open **interview**) approaches. Data gained with the interview technique are coded in words and/or numbers.

Examples are: attitude towards sport; anxiety in skiing; sociometric analysis in sport groups; knowledge test in swimming; interview with the members of the parliament's committee for sport.

(d) Apparatus oriented techniques of data collection.:
This is a rather inhomogeneous group of techniques of data collection. Observation is in these cases realised with the help of apparatus. The techniques of data collection under this category mainly relate to sport medicine and sport biomechanics. Apparatus-oriented techniques of data collection are mostly applied when **parameters of human movement** (motor tests/fitness tests/skill tests) are assessed. In this case sport equipment is often needed and counts as apparatus for the test administration.

Examples are: video recorder to observe sport instruction/training; measurement device for heart rate, blood pressure, etc.; anthropometry; electromyography; dynamometry; kinemetry (kinematography); tests to measure sensory abilities (e.g., vision tests); tests to measure conditional abilities (e.g., COOPER-test); tests to measure coordinative abilities (e.g., reaction-time test); tests to measure technical skills (e.g., slalom-run in soccer); tests to measure tactical skills (e.g., game observation with a video-recorder); tests to measure body experience (e.g., space perception).

A development of categories always provokes some overlapping, since a clear-cut distinction is often not possible. However, the existence of a category system allows for a more comprehensive look at the issue of techniques of data collection. In this way it is also easier to identify those areas, where it is necessary to develop new sport-specific techniques of data collection. This relates especially to the development of tests which take the discussion within measurement-, scaling- and test theory into account (SIXTL 1967; LIENERT 1969; ORTH 1974; BÖS & ROTH 1978; GIGERENZER 1981; KLAUER 1987; ROST 1988; SAFRIT & WOOD 1989).

3.5. Techniques of Data Analysis

The analysis of gained data is the next step in the logic research process. The **data are coded in words** (eventually letters) **and/or numbers.** Often the coding of data in words is not mentioned at all; numbers and consequently statistics generally receive full attention. The concept of research methodology contained in the KMRM, however, subscribes to the continuum idea with two poles. In this case these two poles are numbers and words. Therefore, **two distinct techniques of data analysis** are included in the KMRM.

(a) Non-numerical techniques of data analysis (hermeneutics):
It is often assumed that these techniques are widely known, that the analysis of words is quite easy, and that action-guidelines for analysing words are not necessary. In short: everybody can analyse texts as compositions of words. In practice, however, it can be observed that the application of hermeneutical, non-numerical procedures is quite complex and difficult (KLAFKI 1977; LAMNEK 1988, 1989; GELDSETZER 1989).
The **following procedural steps** have to be taken: realizing of interpretations, making deductions by establishing relationships of 1st and 2nd degrees of order; making summaries; theory building by means of hermeneutical, non-numerical techniques of data analysis is still evolving within sport science. More basic research in regard to research methodology for sport science is urgently needed in this direction (MAYRING 1985; MEINBERG 1987; STRAUß & HAAG 1994).

(b) Numerical techniques of data analysis (statistics):
Many general publications on statistics are available; they relate to descriptive as well as inferential aspects of statistics (STRAUß 1990, 432-453). From a sport-specific point of view relevant books have been published in German (compare: WILLIMCZIK 1975; STEMMLER 1980; BÖS 1986, STEMMLER 1987, 249-296; GENSEL 1987, 231-248; FLEISCHER 1988) and in English (MOREHOUSE & STULL 1975; SAFRIT 1990). Furthermore, the increased usage of computers has opened new avenues in the indicated direction (CICCIARELLA 1986; DONNELLY 1987).
The specificity of the concept within step five of the KMRM is the **combination of numerical/statistical** (STEGMÜLLER 1969-1974; HACKING 1965; BORTZ 1985), and **non-numerical/hermeneutical** techniques on the level of data analysis. This implies again the continuum paradigm with two poles mentioned. Equal

judgement and competence in applying these two aspects of data analysis is also necessary, since with the usage of more than one technique of data collection (compare **triangulation**) it is most likely, that research data are coded in words and numbers.

3.6. Concluding Phase of the Research Process (Knowledge Transfer)

In step six of the KMRM the circle or cybernetic loop is closed and brought back to step one, beginning with the concept of **"practice-guided theory"** (in regard to the finding of assumptions or hypotheses for the research) and ending now with the concept of **"theory-guided practice"**, this means **knowledge transfer**. While in step one the question was "why the given research project" is undertaken, the question in step six is: **"how can the results be transferred to practice?"**

Step six of the KMRM "knowledge transfer" (also knowledge-practice, application theory) is exactly the concretisation of the *"Verwertungszusammenhang"* (application dimension: FRIEDRICHS 1973) within the logic research process. (Solutions to the questions in the basic assumptions or hypotheses are presented to other scholars.) This could be done by publishing the results, giving lectures, attending workshops or other means of publication. The idea is "theory-guided practice", this means the understanding, the conserving, or the developing of practice, if the scientific results and the connected normative-ethical responsibility allow for a transfer of these results. This ethical responsibility is given by intention, since it is not possible, that there is knowledge transfer for the knowledge transfers sake. Not every research result should or can be transferred to practice; examples for such research results are given in nuclear research, environmental research, or sport science research (e.g., doping).

The quest for direct application-orientation of sport science research results cannot mean, that the so-called basic research, which has an indirect application orientation, is neglected. Such basic research is necessary (example: developing a physical fitness test), so that application-oriented research (example: assessing the physical fitness of elementary school children) can be realised with high quality (DOSE 1991, 281-291).

"Theory-guided practice" can be a sensible and appropriate request in the sense of "knowledge transfer". If the practice of sport is further developed, impulses can be derived for step one in the KMRM; this means, that theory can be a **"practice-guided theory"** as starting point for sport science research by providing hypotheses and assumptions. New sport scientific research processes can then be initiated, which, if following the indicated logic research process, can lead to the necessary knowledge transfer (For a detailed description of the transfer paradigm in sport science compare chapter 4 of this analysis).

Conclusion

Research methodology or the question: **"What is the process of gaining scientific knowledge?"** is one of the four classical questions of scientific theory in general but is also important for sport science in specific. The **following points** summarise the analysis of the **KMRM** and thus illustrate the new concept of research methodology for sport science developed in this analysis.

(a) The **six steps** of the KMRM have to be seen as a **logic research process**, which is fundamental to every scientific investigation, no matter whether the investigation has a theoretical or empirical orientation.

(b) The KMRM is **action oriented**, this means, that it describes the steps, which have to be followed, if engaging in processes to gain scientific knowledge, which again could be finalised with a thesis (Master, Doctor).

(c) The single steps of the KMRM are conceptualised in a way, so that they are **valid for any kind of research**. This is reached by implying the **continuum paradigm** with two poles and many variations in between. At the same time it can be avoided, that two basic research approaches, like theoretical and empirical, are seen as completely separate approaches.

(d) The KMRM is an **open model**, since the continuum paradigm allows to integrate new knowledge in regard to research methodology at the different steps. Therefore, the model is not dogmatic or static but rather flexible and dynamic, which appears to be a necessary prerequisite in the field of science.

(e) The overall character of the model implies that scientific endeavours are carried out whith **responsibility towards society**. Therefore, the gaining of scientific knowledge begins with an orientation towards the preconditions and responsibility for the field of sport (HÄGELE 1982) **(practice-guided theory)** and ends with a possible application of the research results in practice **(theory-guided practice)**.

The KMRM is one possibility for model-building in regard to research methodology or sport science. Thus, it is also a contribution towards developing a philosophy of a meta-theory of sport science. This in turn is necessary, so that the many new challenges can be met by science in general, by sport science in specific, and by the different theory- and subject fields of sport science in detail (for sport pedagogy compare HAAG 1983; BREHM & KURZ 1987; PIÉRON & CHEFFERS 1988; for sport sociology compare LENK & LÜSCHEN 1976). In this manner sport science in the search for its identity (WILLIMCZIK 1992, 7-36) may become an interdisciplinary sport science (WILLIMCZIK 1985, 9-32; HAAG 1991b, 292-306; HAAG, KIRSCH & GRUPE 1992).

4. Knowledge Transfer in Sport Science. Or: What is the "Practice-Theory and Theory-Practice" Paradigm?

Introduction

Complaints are often raised that research results are not transferred to practice, that there is a big **gap between theory and practice as well as between practice and theory**. At least in the long-range perspective research can only be justified, if research results are applied. Even so-called fundamental research has an application perspective, since often this fundamental research (e.g., development of a fitness test) is a prerequisite for applied research (e.g., analysis of the fitness of elementary school children in a certain region).

If the requirement of knowledge transfer is discussed within sport science, the **concept of practice** has to be seen **threefold**:

First of all, **practice means physical activity, physical exercise, movement, motor patterns**, etc. "Bewegung" (movement) as the outside perspective and "Motorik" (motor behaviour) as the inside perspective represent the basic nucleus, core or subject matter of our field. This type of practice can have many dimensions. Taxonomies for representing movement/motor behaviour have been developed in order to explain the variability of this practice dimension. Two examples shall illustrate this:

a) The motor domain can be distinguished in the following aspects: anthropometric prerequisites; sensory abilities; conditional abilities; coordinative abilities; body perception; technical motor skills; tactical motor skills.

b) The sport skills, in other words the practical sport disciplines, can be distinguished in the following way: moving of the own body (e.g., track and field); moving of a piece of equipment (e.g., basketball); moving of an object with a piece of equipment (e.g., tennis); moving at a fixed apparatus (e.g., gymnastics); moving due to external forces (e.g., wind surfing).

These two examples already give an indication of the large variety in regard to a necessary transfer of knowledge to this type of practice, namely movement and motor behaviour.

Another dimension of practice, which is of interest in the "practice-theory and theory-practice" paradigm, is the **sport-related professional performance**. For a long time this sport-related professional performance consisted of **teaching physical education** in government institutions, especially schools (distinguished according to age levels or types of schools). Today teaching physical education and coaching sports has been extended to many places outside of governmental institutions (e.g., sport clubs, YMCA's, fitness studios, tourism).

Furthermore, many **non-teaching sport-related professional fields** have evolved (e.g. sport and administration; sport and economy; sport and mass media; sport and recreation; sport and health). Thus, there is an increasing need for generating scientific knowledge in connection with the constantly enlarging practical area of sport-related professional performance, to which knowledge needs to be transferred.

A third dimension of practice in the context of transfer of knowledge is practice understood as the **realisation of the complex social phenomena of movement, play and sport**. It is the task of a responsible research concept to initiate, carry out, and evaluate research related to this form of reality. Research can be initiated by the researcher and by outside request. If sport science takes on this responsibility very carefully, then a large amount of research is carried out, resulting in many theories, which in turn have to be transferred into this type of practice, namely movement, play, and sport. In this way, realities related to movement, play and sport can be better understood in their development and present status, controlled, and possibly changed in the future if necessary. This third dimension of practice, to which transfer of knowledge takes place, is a very comprehensive one in other words it has many aspects.

In summary, it appears as if transfer of knowledge or **"the practice-theory and theory-practice" paradigm** constitutes a very important and necessary aspect of the theoretical foundation of sport science as a scientific discipline.

4.1. From Theory to Practice Understood as Physical Activity

On the one hand, sport science is related also under the label of movement science or kinesiology to movement as a basic behaviour dimension of man. On the other hand, sport science is connected to concrete movements in sport disciplines like swimming (individual sport), badminton (dual sport), and basketball (team sport).

In order to illustrate the wide variety of physical activities four German terms are defined, since this refers directly to the two taxonomies for practice as physical activity, which are presented in this section:

"Eigenschaft" - trait stands for the basic **characteristics** of men in regard to condition and coordination (e.g., endurance or balance).

"Tätigkeit" - **activity** stands for basic motor patterns, which are realized in activities as in the daily routine, work, and leisure time (e.g., throwing).

"Fertigkeit" - **skill** stands for movements in technical and tactical relation connected to sport disciplines (e.g., jump shot in basketball).

"Fähigkeit" - overall mastery stands for **ability** as the combination of trait, activities, and skills (technical and tactile) in order to master a sport discipline like skiing, playing tennis, or playing volleyball.

Within the sport scientific literature a discussion of these terms has been led continuously (e.g., BEYER 1987; EBERSPÄCHER 1987; HAAG 1987a; RÖTHIG 1992; ANSHEL 1991). This discussion cannot be analysed here. The two taxonomies presented in the following examples only give an idea, how variable and complex physical activity as practice can be. Consequently, this practice dimension then has many fales and needs the transfer of knowledge gained in sport science.

4.1.1. Seven-Dimension Taxonomy for the Motor Domain of Human Behaviour

The **seven dimensions** are listed in the order of basic aspects up to complex components of motor behaviour. They cannot always be distinguished sharply and there is overlapping within the taxonomy. The following figure indicates the different levels of the taxonomy:

	1. anthropometric pre-requisites	
	2. sensory abilities	
3. conditional abilities		4. coordinative abilities
	5. body experience	
6. technical motor skills		7. tactical motor skills

Fig. 13:   Taxonomy for the Motor Domain (HAAG 1991a, 78-97)

(1) **Anthropometric prerequisites**: These are the preconditions necessary for performing movement, especially in sport. Two kinds can be distinguished:

-   **Endogenous**, process-oriented physiological parameters (e.g., indicators for breathing; heart rate; blood pressure; body temperature).
-   **Exogenous**, product-oriented body shape parameters (e.g., height, weight, length of extremities; trunk size; skin fold; step length; static flexibility of legs and trunk; spine position; posture of the back, legs, feet).

There are two scientific sub disciplines of sport science related to these parameters: **sport physiology** and **sport anthropometry**. In recent years these prerequisites for movement (including socio-cultural conditions) have been accepted more widely due to the importance of these aspects for the realisation of movement. Consequently the presented taxonomy for the motor domain of human behaviour includes anthropometric prerequisites as its first dimension.

(2) **Sensory abilities**: The importance of the sensory system for movement, play, and sport has been discussed in Germany especially in the sensorimotor theory of UNGERER (1977). The name refers directly to the theory: Movement is composed of sensory input and motor output. Both are connected in a cybernetic loop, which is the basis for cybernetic information theory.

There are **four kinds of receptors** to get information from inside the body and from outside: **telereceptors** (outside of the body surface, e.g., smell organs); **exteroreceptors** (on the skin, e.g., temperature); **interoreceptors** (inside the body, e.g., feeling one's own pulse); **proprioreceptors** (posture- and movement apparatus, e.g., position of body parts) (EBERSPÄCHER 1987, 537-547).

Four sensory abilities are distinguished, which play an important role in sport: **visual ability** (seeing; example: ball games); **auditive ability** (hearing; example: rhythmical callisthenics with the combination of music and movement); **tactile ability** (touching senses; example: in judo for recognising the attacks of the opponent); **kinaesthetic ability** (to experience space, time, and tension conditions within one's own body; e.g., position in springboard diving).

According to EBERSPÄCHER (1987, 539 - 540), **four** general **aspects of per-ception** sensory inputs are very important within sport. Visual perception of objects/movement, processes of the orientation regulation, processes of social perception, and self-perception especially needed in top-level performance. Thus, sensory abilities open a wide field in the practice of sport, which has been neglected all too often so far in sport science research.

(3) **Conditional abilities**: Condition stands for physical performance ability for producing sportive performances. **Endurance, flexibility** (static), **strength**, and **speed** are four main conditional abilities. One differentiates between a general condition and condition related to a specific sport discipline. Conditional abilities mostly exist as so-called complex abilities, e.g., strength-endurance, speed-strength, speed-endurance. This indicates that it is always difficult to get taxonomies without overlaps. Within the scope of this book a closer explanation of the four conditional factors endurance, flexibility, strength, and speed is not given. Extensive discussion on this topic can be found in the literature (e.g., LETZELTER 1978, 161-187). Within the explanation of the transfer paradigm this can be neglected at this point, since the main intent is to illustrate the variability and complexity of physical activity as practice, as summarised in figure 14.

(4) **Coordinative abilities**: In general coordination means the working together of different things or procedures. Within physiology coordination in a more narrow sense stands for the cooperation of the central nervous system and the muscles producing forces. One can distinguish intra-muscular coordination (between nerve and muscle) and inter-muscular coordination (between several muscles). In a broader sense coordination is the name for several abilities, which support the working together of different movement processes. In regard to the learning of coordination one can make the gross differentiation into coordination (motor learning ability), fine coordination (motor control ability) and stabilised fine co-ordination (motor adaptation and change ability) (MEINEL & SCHNABEL 1987, 8). Thus, coordination is closely related to visual-sensory stimulation, sensation of position and balance, and kinaesthetic sensation.

In the sport science literature many models for a differentiation of coordination have been developed (e.g., FLEISHMAN 1964; HIRTZ 1964; MATTAUSCH 1973; MESTER 1988; ROTH 1982).

In the following only **four factors of coordination** are mentioned; the intent is to indicate that not only condition but also coordination can be differentiated: **balance** (mainly situated in the vestibular apparatus); **motor combination ability** (perform simultaneous and successive movements); **agility** (fine and gross coordination; balance; trunk flexibility; adaptation to apparatus, music, and other people); **reaction ability** (stimulus reception; stimulus differentiation; development of an action plan; motor response).

Relative Maximal ↑Strength↑	→	Strength Endurance	←	Endurance
	Speed Strength		Speed Endurance	
	↖	Speed ↓	↗	
	↖ ↙	Movement Speed	↗ ↘	
	cyclic		acyclic	
Sprint strength (within condition)		Spring speed (reaction speed) ↓		Sprint endurance (within coordination)
	↙	Flexibility	↘	
	Static General Passive		Dynamik Specific Active	

Fig. 14:   Structural Model of Conditional Abilities (HAAG 1991, 88)

The very complex construct of coordination can be summarised in the following figure:

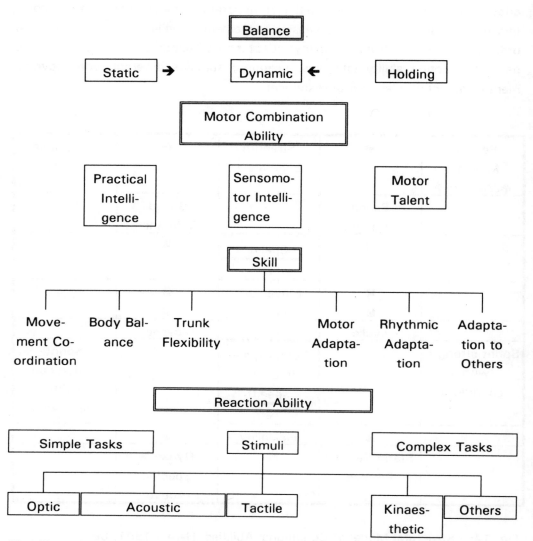

Fig. 15: Structural Model of Coordinative Abilities (HAAG 1991a, 94)

(5) **Body experience**: This is the sum of all experiences with the own body during the life of a human being. GRUPE (1982) has been most productive in an anthropological-philosophical analysis and interpretation of the human body and its possibilities to make experiences, especially primary experiences. BIELEFELD (1986) has developed a model of body experience, seen in two major aspects with some further differentiation, as indicated in figure 16:

Body Experience
Sum of all experiences made within the individual and social development of the own body, being cognitive or affective, conscious or unconscious

Body Scheme
Neurophysiological aspect of body experience, comprising all perceptive-cognitive performances of the individual in regard to the own body

Body Image
Psychological-phenomeno-logical aspect of body experience comprising all emotional-affective performances of the individual in regard to the own body

Body orientation
Orientation in and at the own body with outside and inside sensibility, especially kinaesthetic perception.

Body Consciousness
Psychological representation of the own body or its parts in the individual's mind or the attention directed towards the own body.

Body Size Estimation
Estimation of size and space dimensions of the own body.

Body Boundary
Experience of the body boundaries; the own body in distinction of the environment.

Body Knowledge
Factual knowledge of the build and function of the own body and its parts including the right-left distinction.

Body Attitudes
Total attitude towards the own body and its appearance, especially body satisfaction (or dissatisfaction).

Fig. 16: Structural Model of Body Experience (BIELEFELD 1986, 17)

Similar to aspect (1) (anthropometric prerequisites) aspect (5) (body experience) has also been neglected for a long time in the development of taxonomies for motor behaviour (physical activity). By including this aspect it is especially possible to consider **daily routine-, work-, and leisure time oriented motor patterns** in the development of a comprehensive model for the practice of physical activity (FUNKE 1983).

(6) **Technical motor skills**: These are related very closely to the sport disciplines such as swimming, tennis, or volleyball. If the taxonomy is further differentiated in regard to point (6) models for structuring movement can be used.

GROSSER (1978) differentiates in three directions in his model: skills to change the position of body in space; skills to change the position of the body parts in relation to each other; skills to change the speed and thus the state of movement by applying strength.

GÖHNER (1987) has developed five categories which may be used to structure technical motor skills as the basis of sport disciplines:

- Aim of the movement, solving of a movement task: process-oriented: gymnastics; product-oriented: long jump; both: ski jump.
- Movement object: own body (track and field); partner (dance); opponent (judo); object (basketball).
- Signs of the movement system: natural movement (running); instrumentally supported movement (tennis); movement supported by partners (volleyball).
- Conditions of the environment: inside (gymnastics); outside (soccer); water (sailing); snow (downhill).
- Rules and regulations: constitutive rules and regulative rules and the respective motor skills.

Besides these general theories, which can serve as a basis for building a taxonomy for technical motor skills, differentiations, such as the following, can be used to build categories for technical motor skills:

- open movements (team games) --------- closed movements (discus throw)
- cyclic movements (running) --------- acyclic movements (javelin throw)

In summary, these different possibilities show how variable and multidimensional technical motor skills are.

(7) **Tactical motor skills**: Tactics refer to the optimal and effective usage of technical motor skills on the basis of respective motor abilities in order to realise the basic idea of a sport discipline. Tactical motor skills related to these sport disciplines can be structured according to several criteria. One prerequisite for doing so is the assumption that tactical motor skills are part of the realisation of

every sport discipline and not only of games like often stated. Possibilities for categorisations are:
- Offensive- and defensive tactical patterns.
- Individual-, group-, and team tactics.
- Tactics for certain positions (e.g., goalkeeper, wing player).
- Tactics for the start, the middle, and the end of a competition.

Even if tactical motor skills are based on a combination of motor and cognitive factors, tactics are ultimately realized by mean of motor patterns.
Therefore, it is justified to use "tactical motor skills" as a 7th dimension in the development of a taxonomy for the motor domain of human movement.

4.1.2. Example of a Taxonomy for Sport Disciplines in Five Dimensions

There are many possibilities for describing physical activity in light of the sport disciplines as the major part of the sport reality (and sport practice). Some examples are:
- **Alphabetical** order by simply listing the sport disciplines from 1 to n.
- Differentiation according to **groups** of sport disciplines: e.g., winter sports.
- **Social relation**: individual (track and field), dual (table tennis), and team sports (hockey).
- **Performance assessment**: measurement of performance (cm, gr, sec sport disciplines - swimming); judging of performance (artistic sport disciplines - synchronised swimming); counting of performance (game sport disciplines - water polo).
- **Environment relation**: inside (gymnastics), outside (soccer), water (rowing), snow (cross-country skiing), ice (speed-skating).

Another possibility for structuring sport disciplines in **five dimensions** is given in the following. These dimensions are closely related to the **kind of movement** that is performed and the environmental factors to be considered (e.g., GÖHNER 1987; HAAG 1986a).
(1) Sport disciplines (sub disciplines) where the own body is moved from one place to another (e.g., running in track and field).
(2) Sport disciplines where a piece of equipment is moved (e.g., basketball) in coordination with the movement of the own body.

(3) Sport disciplines where a piece of equipment is moved (e.g., tennis ball) with the help of a medium (e.g., tennis racket).

(4) Sport disciplines where the body is moved on an apparatus (e.g., gymnastics), recognising the socio-cultural and historical variations of the apparatus.

(5) Sport disciplines where external forces move the body (e.g., wind surfing).

The five dimensions are organized in a somewhat logic order from relatively simple movements (1) to very complicated ones (5). Therefore, the last group (5) can also be called risk sport disciplines, which are quite common today. From an educational point of view it is favourable, if people make experiences with at least one sport discipline out of each of the five dimensions: thereby, one can get a feeling for the large diversity of sport disciplines available.

Practice understood as physical activity has been presented as a complex system, which offers many opportunities to generate hypotheses for which an answer is needed. In the same way there is a wide field for application of research results (theories) to the practice of sport, which is a central requirement of a philosophy of science (meta-theory) developed in this study.

4.2. From Theory to Practice Understood as Sport Related Professional Performance

The second dimension of practice analysed in connection with the transfer of knowledge in sport science can be distinguished in **three professional areas** (HAAG & HEINEMANN 1987): **teaching physical activities in state education institutions, in non-state institutions or other teaching/coaching institutions, and non-teaching sport-related professions**. These professional areas developed step by step in this century and today have a different level of professionalisation, length and requirements of the professional training, as well as variety of opportunities. The development of all these professions has to be seen within the large shift in the type of professions. Formerly, many people worked in agriculture; then the industrialisation provided more and more jobs in industry in order to produce goods, which resulted in people moving to the big cities with all the well-known positive and especially also negative side-effects. Recently, a third shift is taking place from the production sector to the area of service professions. In the countries with industry and high technology many people have enough products and goods; therefore, capacities for services are set free. The majority of sport-related professions belong to these service-oriented professions. Therefore, the future perspectives for employment in this area of sport can be seen relatively optimistic.

For these professional opportunities a wide variety of professional training models have been developed, reaching from weekend courses up to a full time university study with an academic examination and qualification. If research results and theory will be transmitted to this sport-related professional practice all these different professional opportunities have to be considered. The **transfer to professional practice can be realized in three settings:**

- **Professional training** ("Ausbildung"), this means receiving a professional licence on different levels.
- **Continued training** ("Fortbildung"), this means updating within one´s learned professional area mainly through courses, short-term workshop, etc.
- **Additional training** ("Weiterbildung"), this means to acquire another qualification in addition to the one for which one is already trained. This form is realized more and more due to the fast changing job requirements and job market with new professions originating and traditional professions disappearing.

The sport-related professional field as a practice field, to which research results and theory may be applied, has to observe another distinction which is made according to the **degree of earning money**. Three patterns characterise the work reality in the field of sport, sport education, and sport science (Winkler 1988).

a) **Honorary work:** Especially within sport clubs and sport organisations honorary work ("Ehrenamt") has had a long tradition and represents a major work force and opportunity for many people for social identification. The work is done without payment, only for expenses such as travel cost, sometimes allowance for food and/or accomodation and some exemptions from taxes. The German Sport Federation ("Deutscher Sportbund") has approx. 25 million members in about 85000 sport clubs; they only can exist due to the help of honorary personnel in teaching ("Übungsleiter"), coaching ("Trainer"), and administering the sport club ("Funktionär"). The requirements for good professional qualification are constantly increasing for this type of work; therefore, the German Sport Federation has founded a special Academy ("Führungs- und Verwaltungsakadmie des Deutschen Sportbundes" in Berlin) to offer the three types of training mentioned above (professional, continued, additional). Consequently, the transfer of knowledge in sport science to professional practice is constantly expanding.

b) **Part-time work:** Several social trends can be observed, which are responsible for part-time work becoming more and more popular also in sport-related professions. Examples for such trends are: the desire of both men and women to work in addition having a family with children; increased demand for raising the standard of living; an increased need to organize professions in a flexible way, especially in the service profession; changing of professional patterns over time and, therefore, change of profession in one's professional life; non-professional settings cannot afford full-time personnel, which frequently results in the pattern, where a person has a second half-time position of a different kind. The professional field of sport provides more and more work opportunities due to the aforementioned reasons on a part-time basis.
The professional requirements are also increasing constantly and there is a wide variety of special licences, which one can acquire in regard to a sport-related professional field. Within this part-time setting variety, fluctuation, and different degrees of theory to practice transfer can be observed.

c) **Full-time work:** Finally the usual pattern of full-time positions also applies to the field of sport in the three situations: state education institutions, non-state institutions and other learning places, non-teaching sport-related professions. Due to the rapid development of movement, play, and sport as a social force and due to the establishment of sport as an important social subsystem, the trend towards more and more full-time work professionalisation is a necessary and understandable consequence. This in turn has enhanced the sport science approach and helped to establish a new scientific and academic discipline which provides more and more knowledge (theories), which in turn have to be transferred to the professional practice, especially the one characterized by full-time work.

Considering these characteristics of sport as a practical field in regard to professional work the **three** already mentioned **professional areas** will be described in the following in some more detail.

4.2.1 Teaching Physical Activities in State Education Institutions

There is a large variety of state institutions in which physical activity is taught. Since coaching also involves a teaching-learning process, it can be considered as a form of teaching.

Examples for state education institutions are:
- **Kindergarten** - with the need for much physical activity for an adequate motor development of children.
- **Pre-school education** - with similar requirements like Kindergarten.
- **Primary school** (grade 1-4 or 1-6), the so-called motor learning age or period with the requirement of daily physical education, which is, unfortunately, rarely realized.
- **Secondary I school** (grade 5-10)). At this level there are many different types of schools, depending on the country and even within a country depending on the political philosophies.
- **Secondary II school** (grade 11-12 or 13). There are again different types of school (including vocational schools), often overlapping with higher education.
- **Higher education** with intramural sport, athletic sport and the different professional training tracks up to the examinations in order to become a faculty member in higher education itself.
- Many other **profession-oriented state institutions** besides institutions of higher learning also provide teaching-learning processes in regard to physical activity. Examples are: military, postal service, police, civil guard, prisons.

The list of examples of state institutions, where teaching of physical activity is a professional field (ALLMER & BIELEFELD 1982), shows how large the possibility and also need is for applying the results of sport science research to practice. It also becomes clear that many issues, topics, and questions for sport science research can come from these state-sponsored and education-oriented institutions.

4.2.2. Teaching Physical Activities in Non-State Institutions - other Teaching/Coaching Places

Due to the increasing importance of sport as a subsystem of society, teaching/coaching places outside of state institutions have gained importance. This can be related, on one side, to many institutions and organisations of general nature, and, on the other side, to institutions and organisations with a sport-specific character. In both types teaching/coaching is taking place. In this regard the coaching aspect has to be added since there is a clearly developed professional training for becoming a coach on different levels (C, B, A, Diploma). The professional tracks for becoming a physical education teacher are variable from licences offered by private institutions up to the ones which also entitle to teach in state education settings. The job market is rather flexible and it is, therefore, difficult to ensure that in every professional training the topic of theory-practice and practice-theory relations in regard to sport science is included.

a) **Examples for institutions and organisations of general nature** are: Companies - with sport offerings as part of their setting (industrial/company sport); churches with church-related sport clubs or other forms of sport opportunities; institutions for therapy and rehabilitation, using physical activity as an integral part of their program; sport and tourism, in which certain leisure-time sports are part of the program, e.g., tennis, wind-surfing, sailing, golf, skiing.

b) **Examples for institutions and organisations with a sport-specific character** are the vast number of sport clubs, which contain many teaching/coaching opportunities. These sport clubs are characterized by five main aspects: voluntary membership, independence of the state, orientation according to the interest of the members, democratic decisions, honorary work as a basis for the functioning of the sport club (however, with a trend towards part-time or full-time work). Seven examples for course offerings in these sport clubs show their importance for the realisation of sport offerings for everyone: small children, special groups, handicapped groups, senior citizens, groups for therapy and rehabilitation, sport for women, sport for all. Of course the groups talented in sport and striving for top-level performance are also part of the sport clubs. All of this is the nucleus and traditionally has been the place for sport offerings.

Besides sport clubs **commercial offerings of sport programs** such as fitness centres and sport schools have become major institutions providing opportunities for engaging in sport. This trend is due to the increase in free time (the length of working time during the week is reduced, longer weekends, more vacations, and earlier retirement). Thus many people have more and more time available for increased leisure pursuits. Often it seems as if the traditional sport clubs and the commercial settings would make each other superfluous; the fact that both exist, however, points to a certain need also for these commercialised centres with different infrastructure, course offerings, and time schedule as compared to the sport club.

It becomes clear that a wide variety of teaching/coaching places exists outside of the state-sponsored educational institutions, where theory-based practical professional work can be applied; the necessity to make this gap between theory and practice narrower must be recognised, so that the practice can benefit and theory (research) is dealing with the right questions.

4.2.3. Non-Teaching Sport-Related Professions

The third group of professional opportunities related to sport only has an indirect connection with teaching or coaching sport. These are professions in the "surrounding" of sport, sport education and also partly sport science. There is also a new form of study in the professional training offered in Germany called **"Diplomstudium"**, a study finished with a profession-oriented diploma, and the study with a **master's degree**; these are two different professional tracks to qualifications for working in non-teaching sport-related fields.

The **non-teaching sport-related professions** have developed only recently. They can be summarised in five categories:

1. **Administration and sport**: opportunities in the public sport administration, the self-administration of sport in clubs and organisations at different levels,

and in private initiatives such as marketing, advertisement, tourism, etc. related to sport.

2. **Economy and sport**: the industry producing sporting goods, but also business-like settings connected to marketing, advertisement, service offerings, etc. As mentioned earlier economy has become the new ideology of sport after the political ideology has ceased. This is another reason, why the relationship of sport and economy has to be observed carefully.

3. **Mass Media and sport**: The different media provide a concrete proof for the fact, that sport has become a major factor in many societies, especially the ones characterized by industrialisation and technology. Sport plays a major role in the media; many professional opportunities with relation to sport are found in connection with media. The professionalisation here has just begun. However, the transfer of research results to this part of professional practice related to sport, is also very important since mass media have a high responsibility for shaping the perception and also future development of sport. The field of sport has to be careful to remain an equal partner in this relationship.

4. **Recreation and sport**: sport is at least one major possibility to be applied in this field. Besides the teaching aspect (compare above) there is a large non-teaching aspect within recreation and sport. This relates to administration, management, animation, counselling and advertisement work. Recreation, also in relation to sport, remains a big challenge for the future.

5. **Health and sport**: in this very diversified professional field movement, play, and sport have an important role in regard to prevention, therapy, and rehabilitation. The prevention aspect is taking on a predominant role and thus also creating many sport related professional opportunities.

This second application dimension for transfer of knowledge in sport science is the sport-related professional performance. This is a vast field for application possibilities of results from sport science research. The success of these transfer opportunities largely depends on the extent to which this transfer paradigm is part of the professional training. If future members of sport-related professions are aware of this important dimension of a scientific theory of sport science, namely the need to transfer theory to practice and to receive the right questions for research from practice, then the transfer paradigm is working and the basic function of sport science is realized, namely to understand, improve, and if necessary change practice in regard to sport through sport-related professional work.

4.3. From Theory to Practice Understood as the Complex Social Phenomenon of Sport

The third dimension of practice analysed in connection with the transfer of knowledge in sport science is the most complex one, namely the **total reality of sport as a subsystem of the society** (for GER: DSB 1992; HEINEMANN & BECKER 1986; DSB 1986-1988; GABLER & GÖHNER 1990). This close relationship of sport to its socio-cultural preconditions is also expressed in the sentence of the famous Spanish philosopher ORTEGA Y GASSET "Every society has the sport, which is earned by this society", in other words every sport system has to be seen in light of the respective socio-cultural conditions.

There are several **structural models** available for understanding **sport as a complex system** (GRUPE 1971; DIGEL 1988; HEINEMANN 1990).

Two models developed by the author will be presented in the following, which can provide an indication of what sport is or can be. Both models are oriented toward the administrative and organisational paradigm, which seems to be very practical and understandable.

1. The **first model** for describing the broad **reality of sport** is based on **four questions,** to which certain answers can be given. These answers more or less indicate what sport is as a social reality (HAAG 1986a).

(1) **What is the aim and objective of engaging in sport?**
Answers: performance sport, sport for compensation, competitive sport, health sport, preventive sport, sport for rehabilitation, sport for therapy, etc.

(2) **Who is engaging actively in sport?**
Answers: child sport, school-age sport, youth sport, adult sport, student sport, sport for women, sport for men, sport for seniors, etc.

(3) **Where are people engaging in sport?**
Answers: school sport, club sport, university/college sport, company sport, prison sport, military sport, police sport, etc.

(4) **When are people engaging in sport?**
Answers: early morning sport, break sport, sport after work, weekend sport, vacation sport, recreational sport, professional sport, etc.

It can be stated that every kind of sport can be characterized by an answer to these questions. For example: preventive sport as adult sport as club sport as recreation sport. In other words, the combination of all these terms in different mixtures can give an impression of the great variety of the complex phenomenon of sport.

In one way or another this variety of forms to realise sport is fascinating, since it shows the diversity of sport in reality. One should, therefore, not take "pars pro toto" and only consider, e.g., top-level-athletics in order to make an evaluation of sport as a social phenomenon. Sport has indeed so many faces, that it is always necessary to name the sport, which is meant in a certain context.

2. The **second model** to describe the broad **reality of sport** is based on a **structural model** for the organisational approach to sport. **Five large sections** are distinguished in this model. They are seen as separate categories in the following; however, in reality there are many relationships between the five sections, especially if one considers the five sections under a longitudinal dimension.

4.3.1. Professional Sport - Show Sport

This is the sport which is practised mainly for earning a living. In the history of sport an increasing tendency can be observed towards professionalism in sport from the Antiquity until today. **Professional sport has certain characteristics**: (1) a short career requires high wages; (2) economics govern sportive aspects; (3) the end of the career in professional sport is often difficult due to the transition to another way of life; (4) the transition from amateur to professional sport is problematic; (5) it is necessary to establish a connection between the professionals and the spectators; (6) negative signs of the show-business also affect professional sport.

It is wrong to consider professional sport as the only form of sport. If it is seen in relation to other forms of sport, watching professional sport events either directly or indirectly (media) can be, in most cases, regarded as valuable.

4.3.2. Sport in Educational Institutions

The educational institutions are quite manifold. They can be **categorised** either according to **levels** (pre-school - elementary, secondary I, secondary II, tertiary, quartiary) or according to **school types** (Kindergarten, primary school, secondary school, middle school, "gymnasium", part secondary school (vocational school), college, university etc). In all these educational institutions sport and physical education plays a certain role which is often much too small, since the majority of educational systems attach a very high value to the cognitive dimension of education and somewhat disregard the motor and affective dimensions. Nevertheless, many forms of sport are realized and therefore all of this is an important part of the sport system, especially since every child experiences this system and therefore gets into contact with movement, play, and sport in one way or another .

4.3.3. Sport in Sport Clubs

Sport clubs are voluntary organisations of people who join together to do sports. One can **differentiate sport clubs**: according to the number of members into small clubs (up to 200), medium sized clubs (200-1000), and large clubs (over 1000); according to the number of sports one, two to six, or more than 7 sports. The sport disciplines practised in sport clubs are organized on different levels beyond the local level: region, state, national, international (HAAG & HEIN 1990, 325-432). **Four major objectives** are supposed to be **realized in sport clubs**: (a) promote individual health and strengthen the vitality of the citizens of a state; (b) contribute to the shaping of the personality and serve educational goals; (c) promote social life through manifold forms of exercising and interaction; (d) provide reasonable and enjoyable forms of spending free time, which is constantly increasing.
Thus, the sport clubs have developed into a very strong part of the total sport system (DSB 1986-1988).

4.3.4. Sport in Commercial Settings

In recent years more and more settings of commercial nature like fitness studios, schools for certain sports, training centers, tourism programs etc. have originated, which offer programs related to movement, play, and sport. Obviously, the offerings in state institutions and in sport clubs were not sufficient or not attractive for the expectations of some people. The **commercial settings** have some **typical characteristics**: flexible timing, international atmosphere, nice surroundings with health-related facilities to be used, instruction and training in a counselling setting. Therefore, this sector of sport offerings is a reality today. A positive effect of this new sector of sport is that it provides new sport related service jobs, which are paid by the people using these services.

4.3.5. Sport in Private Non-Institutionalised Settings

This fifth category sounds sometimes surprising, since it is difficult to grasp it. However, from a sociopsychological point of view it seems important that people also become involved and active on their own private initiative. Life is "overorganized" anyways, and therefore it is important for human development to be able to engage privately and individually in sport. Furthermore, it has to be seen, that the categories (2), (3), and (4) should have the effect, that people are engaging in movement, play, and sport also on their own, after they have learned in physical education classes (2), training groups in sport clubs (3) or tennis-vacations (4) to act in one way or another in sport.

This so called **"private" sport** can be carried out within **individual sports** (sport with oneself), in **dual sports** (sport with a partner) or in **team sports** (sport in a larger group). Thus, private sport in itself has several dimensions and is characterized by a great diversity.

More and more people appear to engage in this private sport, mainly since it is usually easy to organize with respect to time, place, and people. It also is connected to an often heard present-day desire for independence, self-determined acting, and creativity.

These two structural models for the explanation of sport show, that the new understanding of sport science should be a broad one, because there is a responsibility to deal scientifically with the broad area of sport, if science takes its task serious to devote itself to issues of social relevance. All too long sport science or the former theory of physical education has dealt predominantly with school physical education. However, today sport has moved far beyond this aspect, and therefore **four requirements for a scientific theory of sport science,** as developed in this analysis, can be stated:

(a) The **aims and objectives** of sport science have to be enlarged in light of the developments described above.

(b) Consequently the **body of knowledge** of sport science is increasing constantly.

(c) Since there are many different issues and complex topics in need of research in order to get scientifically proven knowledge and answers, the **research methodology** in sport science also has to be improved and developed further.

(d) Finally, an increased **transfer of knowledge** to practice is the consequence of this in order to serve as a sport science which caters to the needs of society.

Conclusion

The theory-practice discussion is as old as philosophic considerations, as long as people have been thinking and thus producing theories as opposed to acting in the sense of practice.

It is important in the **"practice-theory and theory-practice"** paradigm to distinguish two meanings of theory (SEIFFERT 1989, 368-369).

(1) **Theory as the observation of something** as opposed to practice, which means acting and thus changing reality (theory of sport - sport practice).

(2) **Theory as result of scientific work** independent of the method used (either theoretical-hermeneutical or empirical-analytic). Examples are: movement theories, play theories, training theories.

The theory-practice discussion is related to the practice interpretation under (1), namely practice as acting and changing reality and to the theory interpretation under (2), namely theory (ies) as result of scientific work.

Theories, especially scientific theories, may have a long, middle, or short range of application, depending on how strong the scientific proof is. **Practice** may mean - as presented in chapter 4 - actual movement (sport), professional practice, or the social subsystem of sport as a target for research. These distinctions have to be seen, if the practice-theory and theory-practice paradigm is applied.

This **transfer request**, being one of four basic points for a scientific theory (meta-theory) also for sport science, can be **summarised** in the **following points:**

1. **Practice-theory** means that in general assumptions and hypotheses for sport science research have to be generated in connection with practice. Even the so-called pure or fundamental research is connected to some practical determinants, known or unknown. This practice to theory assumption shows that sport science - like other sciences - has a clear social responsibility (see chapter 1. "Aims and Objectives of Sport Science").

2. **Transfer of theory** (gained knowledge) to practice is an important part of the research process. There are several possibilities for realizing this (e.g., publication, workshop, field work). Due to this requirement today the so-called case studies are to be considered as valuable as the representative studies, since the application of results can be realized more directly than with representative studies.

3. **Transfer requires evaluation research**; this means research on the consequences of transfer of theories to practice and on the usefulness of the applied methods of transfer. Since theories as a result of science have also had very detrimental consequences (such as nuclear weapons, chemical weapons, certain products with questionable side effects) "Technologiefolgenabschätzung" (estimation of the consequences of technology) and "Wissenschaftsfolgenforschung" (research that evaluates the consequences of research) is necessary today. This means, that also within sport science evaluation research has to be realized in a much larger extent.
4. In order to be successful in the realisation of the paradigm "practice-guided theory and theory-guided practice" it is necessary to consider the points 1 to 3 already within the **research proposal** (including the financial implications).

If researchers accept this point of view, if it is also acknowledged within the promotion of higher education systems, and if practitioners feel neither underestimated nor not recognised enough by the theoretical world, then the transfer idea can work in reality. Basically, this is a positive outcome of the Marxist philosophy: practice as the start and as the path for theory or the dialectic unity of theory and practice (FETSCHER 1983; HANAK 1976; KOLAKOWSKI 1981). If the **paradigm "practice-theory and theory-practice"** is understood in a socially acceptable dialectic form and not distorted for the advantage of a small ruling power group, then science in general and **sport science** in specific can fulfil a great mission in a **threefold contribution: (I) know about the past**, (II) **understand the present**, and (III) **change things for the future**, where it is necessary. Theory and practice then are not hierarchical, they are a unity contributing to a responsible development of mankind also in the dimension of movement, play, and sport.

Concluding Considerations

The presentation of the study on the **"Theoretical Foundation of Sport Science as a Scientific Discipline"** and the implicit **"Contribution to a Philosophy (Meta-Theory) of Sport Science"** began with "Introductory Considerations"; the purpose was to present the study, the process of investigating, and the logic behind this research theme.

In **four main chapters**, according to four major aspects of scientific theory - **aim and objective/body of knowledge/research methodology/knowledge transfer** - the main research results and consequently the theoretical foundation of sport science were presented.

In the following concluding considerations an attempt is made to summarize the many aspects of this investigation under the three headings:

-- **Theoretical foundations**
-- **Critical evaluation**
-- **Future directions**

Thus, it should be possible to receive comprehensive information on the analyzed issues. This should enable members of the scientific community of sport science to use some of the presented concepts in order to develop and improve sport science.

Theoretical Foundations

The history of science shows that the different sciences have been and are developing over time. KUHN (1967) has named this the change of paradigms in the world of science due to the historical dimension. Therefore, it is important from time to time to do research and analyze the nature and self-understanding of a science like sport science in order to develop the theoretical foundation and to strengthen the character of sport science as a scientific discipline (WILLIMCZIK 1992, 7-36). In philosophy this is discussed on a general level. However, every scientific discipline has to lead this discussion, especially "young sciences" which still have to find their place within the scientific community in general.

The **theoretical foundations** indicate that all four aspects are important for the development of epistemology and scientific theory (meta-theory or philosophy) of sport science. Chapter 1 contains important aspects for the first stage of any research endeavour **(aim and objective)**. Chapter 4 contains the necessary final issues arising after a research process has been carried out **(knowledge trans-fer)**. Chapter 2 **(body of knowledge)** and chapter 3 **(research methodology)** represent the nucleus of this study and also of the meta-theory of sport science. The content of chapters 2 and 3 is the result of several studies of the author related to the topic of meta-theory ("Wissenschaftstheorie") of sport science. Certainly, there are other models available. However, the paradigms offered in this investigation may contribute to theory development in regard to the scientific theory of sport science. The four chapters are logic and systematic within themselves; there is also a logic to the sequence of the four chapters. Therefore, this short summary can be related directly to the conclusions drawn in chapters 1 to 4.

Critical Evaluation

Evaluation is an important process in order to find out about the status of issues and developments. The distinction between input-, process-, and output-evaluation makes it clear, that evaluation can be considered as a basic characteristic of human behaviour (HAAG 1988, 62-76). Thus, it is understandable, that at the end of this study and research project a **critical evaluation** of the **results** has to take place. This can be summarized in the **following points:**

- Since work in regard to **epistemology** ("Erkenntnistheorie") and **scientific theory** ("Wissenschaftstheorie") or meta-theory (philosophy of science) is done relatively seldom, it seems important to also work in this direction in order to constantly develop the scientific basis of sport science.
- Since meta-theory is normally seen mainly in regard to the body of knowledge and research methodology issues, it seems to be necessary to also consider the dimension of **"aims / objectives" and "knowledge transfer"**.
- It has to be mentioned that the **presented models** of the author are offered as **one way,** possible for developing a meta-theory of sport science. They originated as a result of analyzing relevant literature, discussing issues with students and faculty members of sport science institutes, and reflecting on the basis of a theoretical research approach.
- The intention of developing **models** with **structural foundations** for different issues of a meta-theory of sport science can be seen positively in regard to offer understandable paradigms. Negatively it could have the effect of being too narrow and not flexible enough for including unusual and unexpected issues.

- This research approach was influenced by **German** and **North American** con-cepts. Taking concepts of other countries into account can lead to a greater variety regarding models of meta-theory of sport science.
- The frequently asked question, whether **meta-theory** is mainly an **area of general philosophy** or whether it should also be **part of each scientific disci-pline** should not have an exclusive answer; it is part of both.

In summary - as mentioned before - critical evaluation should be a constant process of finding out, what is the status and development of the philosophy or meta-theory of sport science. Thus, it is also possible to get basic information on the **nature and self-understanding of sport science** at a given time.

Future Directions

At the end of this analysis it seems to be legitimate to include some future di-rections with respect to the given topic. By doing so, the paradigm past-pre-sent-future becomes complete. Expressed in a different way, the outcome also of this research study on the "theoretical foundation of sport science as a sci-entific discipline" can be seen in the formulation of "future directions", which is characteristic for a perception of science as included in this study. The future direction will be formulated in line with the structure of this analysis in four major parts. Thus, this final part again is related to the "conclusions", which are drawn directly after each of the four chapters.

The question **"aims, objectives, function"** always has to be asked first before beginning a research procedure or project. It is especially important, that this is clear in the vision of the participating researchers, so that they know why they are doing what they are doing, when and who is involved. The "why" question is the essential one, having consequences for the "what", "when", and "who" question. Two points have to be considered especially in this context:

Firstly, the indication and clear, if possible operationalized formulation of "aims, objectives, function" allows for **evaluation** before, during, and at the end of a process. Therefore, the realization of the concept of evaluation is depending on a clear answer to the why question.

Secondly, the **intrinsic motivation** of participating individuals is enhanced, if they know about the "why". It is most likely, that they are more engaged and show a greater identity with their task; the outcome, therefore, might be a better one than that of a research process where "aims, objectives, and function" are not identified.

In regard to a relatively young science, like sport science, the consideration of this "why" question is of special importance in order to better find its place within the scientific community. A constant reassurance of aims, objectives, and function is, of course, necessary in order to stay in line with developments, to be able to act in a proper way, and not to be urged to merely react. It is also interesting, that the relationship on the time-line "past, present, future" can be seen very clear on these issues and that it makes sense to take "past, present, future" as a valid paradigm, especially within the world of science.

The issue **"body of knowlege"** is a "must" for the understanding of any scientific field. Compare the special issues of the journal "Quest": 3/1987 - Perspectives on Knowledge and Inquiry in Physical Education - (HARRIS & PARK 1987): 3/1990 - Kinesiology (HARRIS 1990). The present time is often characterized by sayings like "the world is increasingly governed by science", "a scientification of our life can be seen", or "science is the key to future developments". There is much truth in these statements and basically every issue, topic, or object can be a target point for science and a starting point for scientific inquiry. This is also the way new scientific fields originate. If a theme, topic, or phenomenon has reached a large amount of social relevance and become an important part of social reality, a scientific discipline is emerging. Examples for such a development are: nutrition, information, waste, environment, or sport sciences. Most often, the plural "sciences" is used, because the topic in consideration only can be scientifically investigated, if several already well-established disciplines work together; consequently, the author has introduces **"theme-oriented sciences"** as a descriptive term for these new scientific disciplines.

Sport science as a "theme-oriented science" depends on the work in the so-called theory fields or subdisciplines of sport science. Within the journal "Sport Science Revue" of ICSSPE the following theory fields were covered in one issue each with a review on the newest development on the international level in regard to research results: Sport medicine (sport physiology)(SHEPARD 1992); sport psychology (SCHILLING 1992); sport sociology (SABO 1993); coaching science (WOODMAN 1993); sport pedagogy (HAAG 1994; compare also HAAG 1992a; 1986b; 1987b; 1989b).

The theme fields of sport science are covered quite intensively in the journal "Quest", the official journal of the "National Association for Physical Education in Higher Education" (NAPEHE) in the USA. Examples are: 2/1990 - Usefulness of motor learning research for physical educators (HARRIS 1990); 2/1992 -

Secondary School Physical Education (SIEDENTOP & SULLIVAN 1992); 1/1993 Ethics in the Study of Physical Activity (THOMAS & GILL 1993).

The question of "body of knowledge", therefore, always has to be considered in a stringent way. A good approach is to develop taxonomies, like the one given in chapter 2, in order to have a comprehensive approach for the content dimension of sport science. By doing this, it is possible to add new issues to the system, the necessary flexibility is guaranteed, and issues are most likely to be formulated on the same level of abstraction. Such **body of knowledge taxonomies** also allow for discovering the "blank spots"; they indicate what scientific research should concentrate on. Last not least it is very important for the students of a scientific discipline to have a good structural knowledge of their field of study. The body of knowledge of sport science will be in constant and intensive development in the future due to the fact, that movement, play, and sport are expanding fields of human life with a great impact on future developments. This implies **cooperation**, **integration** and the acceptance of **interdisciplinary** as a research paradigm (KIRSCH & PREISING 1985, 46-55; de MARÉES & BARTMUS 1985, 56-68; WILLIMCZIK 1985, 9-32; 1992, 7-36).

"Research methodology" is sometimes regarded as an abstract, very theoretical, often not understandable issue, which might even be neglected to a certain extent. The results of this research study in regard to research methodology - presented in chapter 3 - hopefully can show and prove the opposite; namely, that it is indeed important to consider research methodology, in other words questions and issues of how scientifically proven results in form of theories and knowledge can be gained on given topics or themes. With respect to **future directions of research methodology the following points** have to be mentioned.

Firstly, research methodology has developed extensively in recent years in regard to quantity and quality on a **general level**, mainly also within scientific theory or meta-theory as part discipline of philosophy as an academic discipline.

Secondly, since research methodology has many aspects which are accepted and applicable generally in the world of science, the academic discipline of **sport science** has to **be aware** of these new **general developments** and include them in the concept of research methodology for sport science.

Thirdly, at the same time **sport science specific aspects of research methodology** - for example, on the level of "techniques of data collection" - **should be developed** to a high standard and combined with issues of general research methodology.

Fourthly, the research methodology, especially for sport science with a broad range of content from sport medicine up to sport philosophy, must be developed in a balanced way by using a **continuum paradigm**, where both major approaches, namely **hermeneutical-theoretical** and **empirical-analytical**, should be acknowledged including many variations in between these two poles. Thus, the wall between hermeneutics and empirism will hopefully not exist anymore to the same extent in the future.

Fifthly, the **study** concepts at universities will have to shift more and more from transmitting encyclopaedic knowledge to making familiar with strategies, problem-solving procedures, and methods for science-based solutions. Therefore, **issues of research methodology** will play a **larger role** within study curricula, also in sport science. This in turn will upgrade scientific or meta-theory as a topic of research and teaching in general and in sport science in specific.

"Transfer of knowledge" is always mentioned as a requirement and has to do with the old and ever existing problem of the relationship between theory and practice. Just recently the transfer of knowledge of universities, higher education, and research projects has been requested more and more in Germany. Especially in the technological sciences it is required that the consequences of science and research are considered to a greater extent, "Wissenschaftsfolgenforschung", a kind of **evaluation research** has become necessary. The major incentives for this new line of thinking are the political emancipation, the use of public tax money for science, and some very negative consequences of science especially in regard to the issue of environmental control. Therefore, evaluation research will increase in importance up to a real integrated approach, in which the question of the application of research results and the respective consequences are included right from the beginning in the research design, this means from the conceptualization up to the realization aspect of a research project.

In this regard the field of sport has a very interesting, almost **three-dimensional theory-practice situation**; namely sport as practical acting, professional practice, and social reality. The requirement of **"practice-guided theory and theory-guided practice"** therefore has to be regarded especially in sport science. In the future, this requirement has to become an increasingly used criterion for the evaluation of the value of research projects, publications, teaching, and the professional advancement within institutions of higher learning. This importance of knowledge transfer has especially consequences for the reform and development of the study of sport science within institutions of higher education,which relates to undergraduate study (HOFFMAN 1988) as well as to graduate study (HOFFMAN & MORFORD 1987). This change in evaluation criteria for research is necessary, so that a reasonable practice-theory and theory-practice relationship has a real chance in regard to sport and sport science. Since movement, play, and sport exist and since the scientific analysis by help of sport science follows, the reality of sport should, therefore, never be overlooked. Or positively summarized in an expression: **a practice-theory and theory-practice paradigm has to be part of a philosophy (meta-theory) of sport science.**

References

AAHPERD (Ed.). (1991). RQES Forum: Research on Teaching in Physical Education. *Research Quarterly for Exercise and Sport*, 4, 351-387. (With contributions by Morrow, Silverman, Dodds/Placek, Goldberger, Lee, Griffey.)

AAPE (Ed.). (1990). The Evolving Undergraduate Major. *The Academy Papers* No. 23. Champaign.

AAPE (Ed.). (1991). New Possibilities, New Paradigms? *The Academy Papers* No. 24. Champaign.

Abernathy, R. & Waltz, M. (1970). Systematische Wege zu einer Wissenschaft. In H. Haag (Hrsg.), *Die Leibeserziehung in den Vereinigten Staaten*. (179-186). Schorndorf.

ADL (1964). *Die Leistung*. Schorndorf.

Allmer, H. & Bielefeld, J. (1982). *Sportlehrerverhalten*. Schorndorf.

Altrock, H. (1939). *Aufgabe und Umfang der Sportwissenschaft*.

Anders, G. (1984a). Sportsoziologie. In K. Carl u.a., *Handbuch Sport*. (193-231). Düsseldorf.

Anders, G. (1984b). Struktur des Vereinssports. In K. Carl u.a., *Handbuch Sport*. (821-839). Düsseldorf.

Anshel, M.H. (Ed.). (1991). *Dictionary of the Sport and Exercise Sciences*. Champaign.

Ballreich, R. & Kuhlow, A. (Hrsg.). (1980a). *Beiträge zur Biomechanik des Sports*. Schorndorf.

Ballreich, R. & Kuhlow, A. (1980b). Probleme und Lösungsansätze einer Lehr- und Forschungskonzeption der Biomechanik des Sports. *Sportwissenschaft*, 3, 251-281.

Ballreich, R. (1989). Sportbiomechanik. In H. Haag, B.G. Strauß & S. Heinze (Red.), *Theorie- und Themenfelder der Sportwissenschaft*. (18-29). Schorndorf.

Ballreich, R. (1992). Sport Biomechanics: Fundamental Aspects. In H. Haag, O. Grupe & A. Kirsch (Eds.), *Sport Science in Germany. An Interdisciplinary Anthology*. (147-162). Berlin.

Barette, G.T., Feingold, R.S., Rees, L.R. & Piéron, M. (Eds.). (1987). *Myths, Models, Methods in Sport Pedagogy*. Champaign.

Barrow, H.M., McGee, R. & Tritschler, K.A. (1989). *Practical Measurement in Physical Education and Sport*. Philadelphia.

Bauersfeld, K.-H. (1987). Forschungsmethoden in den sportmethodischen Wissenschaftsdisziplinen. *Wissenschaftliche Zeitschrift der Deutschen Hochschule für Körperkultur*, 28, Sonderheft 3.

Baumann, W. (1983). Biomechanik. In P. Röthig (Red.), *Sportwissenschaftliches Lexikon*. (79-80). Schorndorf.

Baur, J. (1988). Entwicklungstheoretische Konzeptionen in der Sportwissenschaft. *Sportwissenschaft*, 4, 391-386.

Becker, P. (Red.). (1983). *Quantitative oder qualitative Sozialforschung in der Sportsoziologie*. Clausthal-Zellerfeld.

Becker, H. & Langenfeld, H. (1983). Sportgeschichte. In P. Röthig (Red.), *Sportwissenschaftliches Lexikon*. (345-346). Schorndorf.

Begov, F. (1980). Einführung in die Geschichte des Sports und der Leibeserziehung der Neuzeit. In O. Grupe (Hrsg.), *Einführung in die Theorie der Leibeserziehung und des Sports*. (24-28). Schorndorf.

Bennett, B., Howell, M., & Simri, K. (1983). *Comparative Physical Education and Sport*. Philadelphia.

Berg, A. & Keul, J. (1992). Exercise Physiology: Fundamental Aspects. In H. Haag, O. Grupe & A. Kirsch (Eds.), *Sport Science in Germany. An Interdisciplinary Anthology*. (37-68). Berlin.

Bernett, H. (1980). Zur Zeitgeschichte der Leibeserziehung und des Sports. In O. Grupe (Hrsg.), *Einführung in die Theorie der Leibeserziehung und des Sports*. (59-87). Schorndorf.

Bernett, H. (1983). Gesundheitserziehung. In P. Röthig (Red.), *Sportwissenschaftliches Lexikon*. (150-151). Schorndorf.

Bernett, H. (1984). Der Beitrag der Sportgeschichte zur Bewußtseinsbildung von Sportpädagogen. *Trendberichte aus der Sportwissenschaft*. (20-27). Schorndorf.

Bernett, H. (1992). Sport History: Sport and National Socialism - A Focus of Contemporary History. In H. Haag, O. Grupe & A. Kirsch (Eds.), *Sport Science in Germany. An Interdisciplinary Anthology*. (439-462). Berlin.

Beyer, E. (Red.). (1987). *Wörterbuch der Sportwissenschaft*. Schorndorf.

Beyer, E., & Röthig P. (1976). *Beiträge zur Gegenstandsbestimmung der Sportpädagogik*. Schorndorf.

Bielefeld, J. (1986). *Körpererfahrungen*. Göttingen.

Bloss, H. (1983a). Sportökonomie. In P. Röthig (Red.), *Sportwissenschaftliches Lexikon*. (351). Schorndorf.

Bloss, H. (1983b). Sportpolitik. In P. Röthig (Red.), *Sportwissenschaftliches Lexikon*. (352-353). Schorndorf.

Böhmer, D. (1984a). Medizinische Betreuung und Beratung im Schul-, Vereins- und Freizeitsport. In K. Carl u.a., *Handbuch Sport.* (941-951). Düsseldorf.

Böhmer, D. (1984b). Sportmedizin. In K. Carl u.a., *Handbuch Sport.* (233-258). Düsseldorf.

Bohus, J. (1986). *Sportgeschichte. Gesellschaft und Sport von Mykene bis heute.* München.

Bortz, J. (1984). *Lehrbuch der empirischen Forschung.* Berlin.

Bortz, J. (1985). *Lehrbuch der Statistik.* Berlin.

Bös, K. (1986). *Statistikkurs I.* Ahrensburg.

Bös, K. (1987). *Handbuch sportmotorischer Tests.* Göttingen.

Bös, K. & Roth, K.D. (1978). Möglichkeiten der Anwendung probalistischer Modelle im Bereich sportmotorischer und sportpsychologischer Forschung. *Sportwissenschaft, 4,* 407-421.

Brehm, W. (1989). Sport und Gesundheit. In H. Haag, B.G. Strauß & S. Heinze (Red.), *Theorie- und Themenfelder der Sportwissenschaft.* (288-301). Schorndorf.

Brehm, W., & Kurz, D. (Red.). (1987). *Forschungskonzepte in der Sportpädagogik.* Clausthal-Zellerfeld.

Brickenkamp, R. (1975). *Handbuch psychologischer und pädagogischer Tests.* Göttingen.

Brickenkamp, R. (Hrsg.). (1986). *Handbuch apparativer Verfahren in der Psychologie.* Göttingen.

Brickenkamp, R. (1993). Erster Ergänzungsband zum *Handbuch psychologischer und pädagogischer Tests.* Göttingen.

Broom, E., Clumpner, R., Pendleton, B., & Pooley, C.A. (Eds.). (1988). *Comparative Physical Education and Sport.* Volume 5. Champaign.

Brüggemann, P. (1984). Biomechanik des Sports. In K. Carl u.a., *Handbuch Sport.* (259-302). Düsseldorf.

Campbell, N. & Stanley, J.C. (1963). Experimental and Quasi-experimental Designs for Research on Teaching. In N.L. Gage (Ed.), *Handbook of Research on Teaching.* (171-246). Chicago.

Carl, K. (1983). Trainingslehre. In P. Röthig (Red.), *Sportwissenschaftliches Lexikon.* (421). Schorndorf.

Carl, K. (1984a). Talentsuche, Talentauswahl und Talentförderung in Schule und Verein. In K. Carl u.a., *Handbuch Sport.* (917-940). Düsseldorf.

Carl, K. (1984b). Training im Wettkampfsport. In K. Carl u.a., *Handbuch Sport.* (305-328). Düsseldorf.

Carl, K. (1989). Trainingswissenschaft - Trainingslehre. In H. Haag, B.G. Strauß & S. Heinze (Red.), *Theorie- und Themenfelder der Sportwissenschaft.* (216-229). Schorndorf.

Carl, K. (1992). Training Science: Fundamental Aspects. In H. Haag, O. Grupe & A. Kirsch (Eds.), *Sport Science in Germany. An Interdisciplinary Anthology.* (223-240). Berlin.

Carl, K. u.a. (1984). Begriffsvielfalt und Systematisierungsproblematik von Sport und Sportwissenschaft. In K. Carl u.a., *Handbuch Sport.* (3-19). Düsseldorf.

Carnap, R. (1959). *Induktive Logik und Wahrscheinlichkeit.* Wien.

Chalmers, A.F. (1986). *Wege der Wissenschaft.* Berlin.

Cicciavella, Ch.F. (1986). *Microelectronics in the Sport Sciences.* Champaign.

Clarke, D.H. & Clarke, H.H. (1970). *Research Process in Physical Education, Recreation and Health.* Englewood Cliffs.

Crum, B. (1988). Zur Entwicklung sportpädagogischer Forschung. *Sportwissenschaft,* 2, 176-184.

Darst, P. W., Zakrajsek, D. B., & V. H. Mancini (1989). *Analyzing Physical Education and Sport Instruction.* Champaign.

DeMarées, H. (1984). Übersichtsbeitrag Sportmedizin. In DSLV (Hrsg.), *Trendberichte aus der Sportwissenschaft.* (92-104). Schorndorf.

DeMarées, H. & Bartmus, U. (1985). Probleme interdisziplinärer Forschung auf dem Gebiet des Sports aus naturwissenschaftlicher Sicht. *Sportwissenschaft,* 1, 56-68.

Denk, H., & Hecker, G. (1981 und 1985). *Texte zur Sportpädagogik.* Teil I/II. Schorndorf.

Dieckert, J. (1983). Freizeitsport. In P. Röthig (Red.), *Sportwissenschaftliches Lexikon.* (139-140). Schorndorf.

Diem, C. (1942). Wissenschaft der Leibesübungen. *Olympische Flamme,* Bd. III. (1273-1275). Berlin.

Diem, C. (1949). *Wesen und Lehre des Sports.* (Vorwort zur 1. Auflage). Berlin.

Diem, C. (1953). Sportwissenschaft als Pädagogik. *Die Leibeserziehung,* 2, 1-2.

Diem, C. (1958). Sport als Wissenschaft. *Deutsche Studentenzeitung,* 8/9, 17-18.

Digel, H. (Hrsg.). (1988). *Sport imVerein und im Verband.* Schorndorf.

Donnelly, J.E. (1987). *Using Microcomputers in Physical Education and the Sport Sciences.* Champaign.

Dordel, S. (1984). Schulsonderturnen (Sportförderunterricht). In K. Carl u.a., *Handbuch Sport.* (773-792). Düsseldorf.

Dose, H.J. (1991). Zum Gegenstand und zur Funktion von Sportwissenschaft. In H. Haag, *Einführung in das Studium der Sportwissenschaft.* (281-291). Schorndorf.

DSB (Hrsg.). (1986-1988). Die Zukunft des Sports. *Menschen im Sport 2000.* Schorndorf.

DSB (Hrsg.). (1992). *Sport in der Bundesrepublik Deutschland.* Frankfurt a.M.

DSLV (Red.). (1967-1994). *Das Studium der Sportwissenschaft.* Wetzlar.

Eberspächer, H. (Hrsg.). (1987). *Handlexikon Sportwissenschaft.* Reinbek.

Erbach, G. (1964). Gedanken zur Einordnung der Theorie der Körperkultur als Lehr- und Forschungsdisziplin in das System der Sportwissenschaft. *Theorie und Praxis der Körperkultur,* Sonderheft: Über philosophische und soz. Probleme der Körperkultur, 74-82.

Erbach, G. (1965). Über die Bedeutung der wissenschaftlichen Perspektivplanung auf dem Gebiet der Körperkultur unter besonderer Berücksichtigung der Grundlagenforschung. *Theorie und Praxis der Körperkultur,* 4, 348-358.

Erbach, G. (1967). Zu wissenschaftstheoretischen Fragen der Sportwissenschaft. *Theorie und Praxis der Körperkultur,* 17, Beiheft: Sportwissenschaftlicher Kongreß vom 23-25.11.1967, Teil III, 120-128.

Erbach, G. (1973). Die Sportwissenschaft und ihre Aufgaben bei der Entwicklung der sozialistischen Körperkultur. *Theorie und Praxis der Körperkultur,* 10, 888-900.

Erbach, G. (1977). Die Aufgaben der Sportwissenschaft mit höherer Qualität lösen. *Theorie und Praxis der Körperkultur,* 6, 407-410.

Erdmann, R. (1988). Die Bedeutung empirischer Studien mit kleinen Stichproben für die Theoriebildung im sozialwissenschaftlichen Bereich. *Sportwissenschaft,* 3, 270-283.

Faßnacht, G. (1979). *Systematische Verhaltensbeobachtung.* München.

Fetscher, J. (1983). *Der Marxismus. Seine Geschichte in Dokumenten.* München.

Fetz, F. (1961). Zum Wissenschaftscharakter der "Theorie der Leibeserziehung". *Leibesübungen/Leibeserziehung,* 3, 1-7.

Fetz, F. (1964). Zum Wissenschaftscharakter der Theorie der Leibeserziehung. In *Beiträge zu einer Bewegungslehre der Leibesübungen.* (11-32). Wien.

Fetz, F. (1966). Zur Theorie der Leibeserziehung und ihrer Gliederung. *Die Leibeserziehung,* 5, 154-162.

Fetz, F. & Kornexl, E. (Hrsg.). (1993). *Sportmotorische Tests.* Wien.

Feyerabend, P.K. (1976). *Wider den Methodenzwang.* Frankfurt/M.

Fleischer, H. (1988). *Grundlagen der Statistik.* Schorndorf.

Fleishman, E.A. (1964). *The Structure and Measurement of Physical Fitness.* New York.

Franke, E. (1992). Sport Philosophy: Key Problems. In H. Haag, O. Grupe & A. Kirsch (Eds.), *Sport Science in Germany. An Interdisciplinary Anthology.* (501-536). Berlin.

Frey, G. (1984). Trendbericht Trainingslehre. In DSLV (Hrsg.), *Trendberichte aus der Sportwissenschaft.* (62-78). Schorndorf.

Friedrichs, J. (1976). *Methoden der empirischen Sozialforschung.* Reinbek.

Fu, F. & Speaks, M. (Eds.). (1989). *Comparative Physical Education and Sport.* Volume 6. Hongkong.

Gabler, H. (1983). Sportpsychologie. In P. Röthig (Red.), *Sportwissenschaftliches Lexikon.* (353-355). Schorndorf.

Gabler, H. & Röthig, P. (1980). Psychologische Grundfragen der Leibeserziehung und des Sports. In O. Grupe (Hrsg.), *Einführung in die Theorie der Leibeserziehung und des Sports.* (111-141). Schorndorf.

Gabler, H. & Göhner, U. (Hrsg.). (1990). *Für einen besseren Sport. Themen, Entwicklungen und Perspektiven aus Sport und Sportwissenschaft.* Schorndorf.

Geldsetzer, L. (1989). Hermeneutik. In H. Seiffert & G. Radnitzky (Hrsg.), *Handlexikon zur Wissenschaftstheorie.* (127-139). München.

Gensel, B. (1987). Mathematisch-statistische Methoden. In K.-H. Bauersfeld (Red.), Forschungsmethoden in den sportmethodischen Wissenschaftsdisziplinen. *Wissenschaftliche Zeitschrift der DHfK, 28,* Sonderheft 3, 231-248.

Gigerenzer, G. (1981). *Messung und Modellbildung in der Psychologie.* München.

Göhner, U. (1983). Bewegungslehre. In P. Röthig (Red.), *Sportwissenschaftliches Lexikon.* (70). Schorndorf.

Göhner, U. (1984). Bewegungslehre. In DSLV (Hrsg.), *Trendberichte aus der Sportwissenschaft.* (28-35). Schorndorf.

Göhner, U. (1987). *Bewegungsanalyse im Sport.* Schorndorf.

Göhner, U. (1989). Bewegungstheorie - Bewegungslehre. In H. Haag, B.G. Strauß & S. Heinze (Red.), *Theorie- und Themenfelder der Sportwissenschaft.* (198-207). Schorndorf.

Göhner, U. (1992). Movement Theory: Fundamental Aspects. In H. Haag, O. Grupe & A. Kirsch (Eds.), *Sport Science in Germany. An Interdisciplinary Anthology.* (191-200). Berlin.

Greendorfer, S. L. (1987). Specialization, Fragmentation, Integration, Discipline, Profession: What is the Real Issue? *Quest, 39,* 36-64.

Groll, H. (1956). Möglichkeiten und Grenzen einer Wissenschaft der Leibeserziehung. *Die Leibeserziehung* 11, 329-334.

Groll, H. (1957). Die Stellung der Wissenschaft der Leibeserziehung zu den Leibesübungen. *Wissenschaft und Weltbild,* 281-288.

Groll, H. (1959). Vom Wissenschaftscharakter der Theorie der Leibesübungen. In J. Recla (Hrsg.). *Bibliographie und Dokumentation der Leibesübungen.* (56-66). Graz.

Groll, H. (1961). Was ist der Forschungsgegenstand der Theorie der Leibeserziehung? *Leibesübungen/Leibeserziehung,* 3, 22-24.

Groll, H. (1973). Sportwissenschaft in Österreich - Erbe und Auftrag. *Leibesübungen/Leibeserziehung,* 5, 104-106.

Grosser, M. (1978). Ansätze zu einer Bewegungslehre des Sports. *Sportwissenschaft,* 8, 370-392.

Grosser, M. & Starischka, S. (1981). *Konditionstests.* München.

Grössing, S. (1979). *Spektrum der Sportdidaktik.* Bad Homburg.

Größing, S. (1992). Sportdidaktik. In P. Röthig (Red.), *Sportwissenschaftliches Lexikon.* (428-427). Schorndorf.

Grupe, O. (1968). Über das Problem einer Wissenschaft oder wissenschaftlichen Theorie der Leibeserziehung. In O. Grupe, *Studien zur pädagogischen Theorie der Leibeserziehung.* (5-34). Schorndorf.

Grupe, O. (1971). Einleitung in die Sportwissenschaft. *Sportwissenschaft,* 1, 7-18.

Grupe, O. (1973). Sportwissenschaft - Aufgaben und Probleme einer neuen Disziplin. *Attempo,* 47/48, 20-26.

Grupe, O. (1977). Sportwissenschaft in der Lehrerbildung und Lehrerfortbildung. *Zeitschrift für Sportpädagogik,* 4, 393-405.

Grupe, O. (1980a). Anthropologische Grundlagen der Leibeserziehung und des Sports: Leib/Körper, Bewegung und Spiel. In O. Grupe (Hrsg.), *Einführung in die Theorie der Leibeserziehung und des Sports.* (88-110). Schorndorf.

Grupe, O. (1980b). Bewegung, Spiel und Sport in der Erziehung - Ziele und Aufgaben. In O. Grupe (Hrsg.), *Einführung in die Theorie der Leibeserziehung und des Sports.* (216-243). Schorndorf.

Grupe, O. (1980c). Sporttheorie in der Sportlehrerausbildung. In O. Grupe (Hrsg.), *Einführung in die Theorie der Leibeserziehung und des Sports.* (11-22). Schorndorf.

Grupe, O. (1982). *Bewegung, Spiel und Leistung im Sport. Grundthemen der Sportanthropologie.* Schorndorf.

Grupe, O. (1984a). Anthropologische Grundfragen der Sportpädagogik. In DSLV (Hrsg.), *Trendberichte aus der Sportwissenschaft.* (79-91). Schorndorf.

Grupe, O. (1984b). *Grundlagen der Sportpädagogik*. Schorndorf.

Grupe, O. (1986). Künftige Aufgaben und Probleme der Sportwissenschaft. In K. Heinemann & H. Becker (Hrsg.), *Die Zukunft des Sports*. Materialien zum Kongreß "Menschen im Sport 2000". (262-268). Schorndorf.

Grupe, O. (1989). Anthropologische Grundlegung der Leibeserziehung. *International Review of Education*, 1, 17-37.

Grupe, O. (1992). Sport Pedagogy: Anthropological Foundations. In H. Haag, O. Grupe & A. Kirsch (Eds.), *Sport Science in Germany. An Interdisciplinary Anthology*. (361-378). Berlin.

Grupe, O., Gabler, H. & Göhner, U. (Hrsg.). (1983). *Spiel - Spiele - Spielen*. Schorndorf.

Grupe, O. & Kurz, D. (1983). Sportpädagogie. In P. Röthig (Red.), *Sportwissenschaftliches Lexikon*. (351-352). Schorndorf.

Grupe, O. & Krüger, M. (1989). Spieltheorie - Spiellehre. In H. Haag, B.G. Strauß & S. Heinze (Red.), *Theorie- und Themenfelder der Sportwissenschaft*. (208-215). Schorndorf.

Guba, E.G. & Lincoln, Y.S. (1988). Naturalistic and Rationalistic Inquiry. In J.P. Keeves (Ed.). *Educational Research, Methodology, and Measurement: An International Handbook*. (81-85). London.

Güldenpfennig, S. (1989). Politikwissenschaft und Sport - Sportpolitik. In H. Haag, B.G. Strauß & S. Heinze (Red.), *Theorie- und Themenfelder der Sportwissenschaft*. (138-159). Schorndorf.

Gutewort, W. & Thorauer, H.-A. (1987). Die Modellmethode. In K.-H. Bauersfeld (Red.), Forschungsmethoden in den sportmethodischen Wissenschaftsdisziplinen. *Wissenschaftliche Zeitschrift der DHfK*, 28, Sonderheft 3, 121-150.

Haag, H. (1970). *Die Leibeserziehung in den Vereinigten Staaten*. Schorndorf.

Haag, H. (1976). Zur inhaltlichen Konzipierung der Sportpädagogik als Aspekt der Sportwissenschaft. In H. Andrecs, & S. Redl, (Eds.), *Forschung, Lehren, Handeln*. (251-276). Wien.

Haag, H., (Ed.). (1978). *Sport Pedagogy. Content and Methodology*. Baltimore.

Haag, H. (1979). Development and Structure of a Theoretical Framework for Sport Science ('Sportwissenschaft'). *Quest,* 31, 25-35.

Haag, H. (Ed.). (1981). *Physical Education and Evaluation*. Schorndorf.

Haag, H. (1982a). Research in Sport Pedagogy: Retrospective and Prospective. *International Journal of Physical Education*, 1, 13-22.

Haag, H. (1982b). Research Methodology in Sport Science: Implications for the Comparative Research Approach. In J.C. Pooley & C.A. Pooley (Eds.),

Proceedings from the Second International Seminar on Comparative Physical Education and Sport. (89-110). Halifax.

Haag, H. (1983). Entwicklung einer Forschungsmethodologie für Sportpädagogik als Theoriefeld der Sportwissenschaften. In M. Reichenbach (Hrsg.), *Sportpädagogik - Körpererziehung - Persönlichkeit.* (53-81). Potsdam.

Haag, H. (1985). Lehrplan- und Unterrichtsthorie des Sports. In H. Denk, & G. Hecker. (Hrsg.). *Texte zur Sportpädagogik.* II. Teil (167-189). Schorndorf.

Haag, H. (1986 a). *Bewegungskultur und Freizeit.* Osnabrück.

Haag, H. (1986b). Relationships of Curriculum and Instruction Theory as Major Aspects of Sport Pedagogy. In M. Piéron, & G. Graham. (Eds.). *Sport Pedagogy.* The 1984 Olympic Scientific Congress Proceedings. Vol. 6. (151-162). Champaign.

Haag, H. (1987a). *Schülerduden "Der Sport".* Mannheim.

Haag, H. (1987b). Sport Pedagogy: An Applied Field of Educational Science and a Theory Field of Sport Science. In: *Seoul Olympic Scientific Congress Organizing Committee,* (Ed.). Better Life through Sports. Proceedings of the 1986 Asian Games Scientific Congress. (353-361). Seoul.

Haag, H. (1988). Auswertung von Lehr- und Lernprozessen im Sport. In C. Cwalina (Hrsg.), *Methodisches Handeln im Sportunterricht.* (62-76). Schorndorf.

Haag, H. (1989a). Research in 'Sport Pedagogy' - one Field of Theoretical Study in the Science of Sport. *International Review of Education,* 1, 5-16.

Haag, H. (1989b). Sportpädagogik. In H. Haag, B.G. Strauß & S. Heinze (Red.), *Theorie- und Themenfelder der Sportwissenschaft* (48-69). Schorndorf.

Haag, H. (1989c). Sportphilosophie. In H. Haag, B. Strauß & S. Heinze (Red.), *Theorie- und Themenfelder der Sportwissenschaft.* (94-123). Schorndorf.

Haag, H. (Ed.). (1989d). Sports and Physical Education. Vol. 35 *International Review of Education,* 1. (With Contributions by: Haag, Grupe, Jewett, Piéron, Kudlorz, Ojeme.)

Haag, H. (1990). Sportwissenschaft in internationaler Sicht - interkulturell-vergleichende Forschungsstrategie und das Beispiel "Sportwissenschaft in den USA". In H. Gabler & K. Göhner, *Für einen besseren Sport.* (308-324). Schorndorf.

Haag, H. (1991a). *Einführung in das Studium der Sportwissenschaft. Berufsfeld-, Studienfach- und Wissenschaftsorientierung.* Schorndorf.

Haag, H. (1991b). Forschungsmethodologie der Sportwissenschaft (Forschungslogischer Ablauf). In H. Haag u.a. *Einführung in das Studium der Sportwissenschaft.* Berufsfeld-, Studienfach- und Wissenschaftsorientierung. (292-306). Schorndorf.

HAAG, H. (1991c). Qualitativ und quantitativ. - Ein falscher Gegensatz in der forschungsmethodologischen Diskussion der Sportwissenschaft. In R. Singer (Hrsg.), *Sportpsychologische Forschungsmethoden. Grundlagen. Probleme. Ansätze.* (69-76). Köln.

Haag, H. (1992a). Sport Pedagogy: Fundamental Aspects. In H. Haag, O. Grupe & A. Kirsch (Eds.), *Sport Science in Germany. An Interdisciplinary Anthology* (329-360). Berlin.

Haag, H. (1992b). Sport Philosophy: Fundamental Aspects. In H. Haag, O. Grupe & A. Kirsch (Eds.), *Sport Science in Germany. An Interdisciplinary Anthology* (463-500). Berlin.

Haag, H. (Ed.). (1994). Sport Pedagogy. Vol. 3. *Sport Science Revue*, 1. (With contributions by Haag, Naul, Grupe/Krüger, Vickers, Schempp/Choi, Jewett, Piéron, Silverman, Kang, Cheffers).

Haag, H. (n.y.). Forschungsmethodologie in der Sportwissenschaft. Grundlagen des vergleichenden Forschungsansatzes. In P. Kapustin (Hrsg.), *Beiträge zu Grundfragen des Sports und der Sportwissenschaft.* (28-40). Schorndorf.

Haag, H., Bennett, B., & Kayser, D. (Eds.). (1986). *Comparative Physical Education and Sport.* Volume 4. Champaign.

Haag, H. & Dassel, H. (Hrsg.). (1991). *Fitness-Tests.* Schorndorf.

Haag, H. & Hein, K. (1990). (Red.) *Informationswege zur Theorie und Praxis des Sports.* Bücher - Schriftenreihen - Zeitschriften - Dokumente - Institutionen und Organisationen. Schorndorf.

Haag, H. & Heinemann, K. (1987). *Berufsfeld Sport.* Schorndorf.

Haag, H., Kirsch, A. & Kindermann, K. (1991). *Dokumente zu Sport, Sporterziehung und Sportwissenschaft.* Schorndorf.

Haag, H., Strauß B.G. & Heinze, S. (Red.). (1989). *Theorie- und Themenfelder der Sportwissenschaft. Orientierungshilfen zur Konzipierung sportwissenschaftlicher Untersuchungen.* Schorndorf.

Habermas, J. (1967). *Zur Logik der Sozialwissenschaften.* Frankfurt/M.

Habermas, J. (1975). *Erkenntnis und Interesse.* Frankfurt a.M.

Hacking, I. (1965). *Logic of Statistical Inference.* Cambridge.

Hagedorn, G. (1983). Spieltheorie. In P. Röthig (Red.), *Sportwissenschaftliches Lexikon.* (326-331). Schorndorf.

Hager, W. & Westermann, R. (1983). Planung und Auswertung von Experimenten. In J. Bredenkamp & H. Feger (Hrsg.), *Hypothesenprüfung. Forschungsmethoden der Psychologie.* Bd. 5. (24-238). Göttingen.

Hager, W. (1987). Grundlagen einer Versuchsplanung zur Prüfung empirischer Hypothesen in der Psychologie. In G. Lüer, *Allgemeine experimentelle Psychologie.* (43-265). Stuttgart.

Hahn, E. & Baumann, W. (1983). Leistung. In P. Röthig (Red.), *Sportwissenschaftliches Lexikon*. (223-225). Schorndorf.

Hahn, E. (1989). Sportpsychologie. In H. Haag, B.G. Strauß & S. Heinze (Red.), *Theorie- und Themenfelder der Sportwissenschaft*. (30-47). Schorndorf.

Hammerer, B. (1984). Zur Organisation des Freizeit- und Breitensports. In K. Carl u.a., *Handbuch Sport*. (841-876). Düsseldorf.

Hammerich, K. & Lüschen, G. (1980). Grundzüge soziologischer Bestimmungen von Leibeserziehung und Sport. In O. Grupe (Hrsg.), *Einführung in die Theorie der Leibeserziehung und des Sports*. (183-214). Schorndorf.

Harris, J.C. & Park, R. (Eds.). (1987). Perspectives on Knowledge and Inquiry in Physical Education. *Quest*, 3.

Harris, J.C. (Ed.). (1990). Usefulness of Motor Learning Research for Physical Educators. *Quest*, 2.

Harris, J.C. (Ed). (1990). Kinesiology. *Quest*, 3.

Hasemann, K. (1983). Verhaltensbeobachtung und Ratingverfahren. In K.J. Groffmann & L. Michel (Hrsg.), *Verhaltensdiagnostik. Psychologische Diagnostik*. Bd. 4. (434-488). Göttingen.

Heinemann, K. (1980). Wissenschaftliche Beratung in der Sportpolitik. Ein Beitrag zum Theorie-Praxis-Problem in der Sportwissenschaft. *Sportwissenschaft*, 4, 360-374.

Heinemann, K. (1983). Sportsoziologie. In P. Röthig (Red.), *Sportwissenschaftliches Lexikon*. (358-359). Schorndorf.

Heinemann, K. (1984). *Texte zur Ökonomie des Sports*. Schorndorf.

Heinemann, K. (1985). Entwicklungsbedingungen der Sportwissenschaft. *Sportwissenschaft*, 1, 33-45.

Heinemann, K. (1987). *Betriebswirtschaftliche Grundlagen des Sportvereins*. Schorndorf.

Heinemann, K. (1989a). Sportsoziologie. In H. Haag, B.G. Strauß & S. Heinze (Red.), *Theorie- und Themenfelder der Sportwissenschaft*. (70-81). Schorndorf.

Heinemann, K. (1989b). Ökonomie des Sports. In H. Haag, B.G. Strauß & S. Heinze (Red.), *Theorie- und Themenfelder der Sportwissenschaft*. (184-197). Schorndorf.

Heinemann, K. (1990). *Einführung in die Soziologie des Sports*. Schorndorf.

Heinemann, K. (1992a). Sport Sociology: Fundamental Aspects. In H. Haag, O. Grupe & A. Kirsch (Eds.), *Sport Science in Germany. An Interdisciplinary Anthology*. (379-402). Berlin.

Heinemann, K. (1992b). Sport Sociology: Socioeconomic Problems of Sport. In H. Haag, O. Grupe & A. Kirsch (Eds.), *Sport Science in Germany. An Interdisciplinary Anthology.* (403-422). Berlin.

Heinemann, K. & Becker, H. (1986). *Die Zukunft des Sports.* Schorndorf.

Henry, F. M. (1970). Physical Education. An Academic Discipline. In H. S. Slusher & A. S. Lockhart (Eds.), *Anthology of Contemporary Readings.* (277-282). Dubuque.

Hildenbrandt, E. (1980). Grundlagen einer schulsportorientierten Trainingslehre. In O. Grupe (Hrsg.), *Einführung in die Theorie der Leibeserziehung und des Sports.* (348-373). Schorndorf.

Hirtz, P. (1964). Zur Bewegungseigenschaft Gewandtheit. *Theorie und Praxis der Körperkultur,* 8, 729-735.

Hirtz, P. (1987). Die empirisch-analytische Methode. In K.-H. Bauersfeld (Red.), Forschungsmethoden in den sportmethodischen Wissenschaftsdisziplinen. *Wissenschaftliche Zeitschrift der DHfK,* 28, Sonderheft 3, 63-88.

Hoffmann, S.J. & Morford, R. (Eds.). (1987). The Future of Graduate Study in Physical Education. *Quest,* 2.

Hoffmann, S.J. (Ed.). (1988). Physical Education and the Reform of Undergraduate Education. *Quest,* 1.

Hollmann, W. (1980). Medizinische Grundlagen der Leibesübungen und des Sports. In O. Grupe (Hrsg.), *Einführung in die Theorie der Leibeserziehung und des Sports.* (316-347). Schorndorf.

Hollmann, W. (1983). Sportmedizin. In P. Röthig (Red.), *Sportwissenschaftliches Lexikon.* (350). Schorndorf.

Hollmann, W. (1989). Sportmedizin. In H. Haag, B.G. Strauß & S. Heinze (Red.), Theorie- und Themenfelder der Sportwissenschaft (6-17). Schorndorf.

Hollmann, W. (1992). Sports Medicine: Fundamental Aspects. In H. Haag, O. Grupe & A. Kirsch (Eds.), *Sport Science in Germany. An Interdisciplinary Anthology* (105-118). Berlin.

Hubbard, H.W. (Ed.). (1973). *Research Methods in Health, Physical Education, and Recreation.* Washington D.C.

Huber, O. (1987). *Das psychologische Experiment: Eine Einführung.* Bern.

Hübner, K. (1978). *Kritik der wissenschaftlichen Vernunft.* Freiburg.

Jewett, A. (1989). Curriculum Theory in Physical Education. *International Review of Education,* 1, 35-49.

Jüger, R.S. (Hrsg.)(1988). *Psychologische Diagnostik.* München.

Jütting, D.H. & Scherer, A. (1989). Freizeitsport. In H. Haag, B.G. Strauß & S. Heinze (Red.), *Theorie- und Themenfelder der Sportwissenschaft* (262-287). Schorndorf.

Kayser, D. (1983). Gesundheitstraining. In P. Röthig (Red.), *Sportwissenschaftliches Lexikon*. (150-151). Schorndorf.

Kayser, D. (1984a). Sportdidaktik. In K. Carl u.a., *Handbuch Sport*. (63-82). Düsseldorf.

Kayser, D. (1984b). Training und Animation im Breitensport. In K. Carl u.a., *Handbuch Sport*. (329-350). Düsseldorf.

Kayser, D., & Preising, W. (1982). *Aspekte der Unterrichtsforschung im Sport*. Schorndorf.

Keeves, J. P. (Ed.). (1988). *Educational Research, Methodology, and Measurement. An International Handbook*. Oxford.

Keppel, G. (1982). *Design and Analysis. A Researchers Handbook*. Englewood Cliffs.

Kerlinger, F.N. (1986). *Foundations of Behavioral Research*. New York.

Kirk, R.E. (1982). *Experimental Design*. Belmont.

Kirkendall, D.R., Gruber, J.J. & Johnson R.E. (1987). *Measurement and Evaluation for Physical Educators*. Champaign.

Kirsch, A. (1984). Probleme des Medieneinsatzes in der Schule. In K. Carl u.a., *Handbuch Sport*. (757-772). Düsseldorf.

Kirsch, A. (1990). Die Olympischen Wissenschaftskongresse. In H. Gabler & K. Göhner, *Für einen besseren Sport*. (325-340). Schorndorf.

Kirsch, A. & Preising, W. (1985). Interdisziplinäre Forschung als praktisches Problem der Wissenschaftsorganisation. *Sportwissenschaft*, 1, 46-55.

Klafki, W. (1977). Hermeneutische Verfahren in der Erziehungswissenschaft. In W. Klafki et.al. *Erziehungswissenschaft*. Frankfurt/M.

Klauer, K.J. (1987). *Kriteriumsorientierte Tests*. Göttingen.

Kleinmann, S. (1968). Toward a Non-Theory of Sport. *Quest*, 10, 29-34.

Kneyer, W. (1989). Informationswissenschaft und Sport - Sportinformation. In H. Haag, B.G. Strauß & S. Heinze (Red.), *Theorie- und Themenfelder der Sportwissenschaft* (126-137). Schorndorf.

Kofler, G. (1983). Gefängnissport. In P. Röthig (Red.), *Sportwissenschaftliches Lexikon*. (145). Schorndorf.

Kraft, V. (1968). *Der Wiener Kreis. Der Ursprung des Neopositivismus*. Wien.

Krebs, D. (1983). Sportpublizistik. In P. Röthig (Red.), *Sportwissenschaftliches Lexikon*. (355-356). Schorndorf.

Kriz, J. & Lisch, R. (1988). *Methodenlexikon*. München.

Krotee, M. , & Jaeger, E.M. (Eds.). (1986). *Comparative Physical Education and Sport*. Volume 3. Champaign.

Krüger, A. & Niedlich, D. (1985). *100 Ballspiel-Fertigkeitstests*.

Krüger, M. (1993). *Einführung in die Geschichte der Leibeserziehung und des Sports*. Teil 2: Leibeserziehung im 19. Jahrhundert. Turnen fürs Vaterland. Teil 3: Leibeserziehung im 20. Jahrhundert (Sport für alle). Schorndorf.

Kudlorz, P. (1989). Comparative Physical Education: An International Scientific Approach. *International Review of Education*, 1, 65-72.

Kuhn, T.S. (1967). *Die Struktur wissenschaftlicher Revolutionen*. Frankfurt/M.

Kunath, H. (1988). Differenzierung und Intergration in der Sportwissenschaft. In *Theorie und Praxis der Körperkultur*, 6, 366-373.

Kurz, D. (1979). *Elemente des Schulsports. Grundlagen einer pragmatischen Fachdidaktik*. Schorndorf.

Kwiatkowski, G. (1985). *Schülerduden Philosophie*. Mannheim.

Lamnek, S. (1988). *Qualitative Sozialforschung*. Band I. Methodologie. München.

Lamnek, S. (1989). *Qualitative Sozialforschung*. Band II. Methoden und Techniken. München.

Langenfeld, H. (1989). Sportgeschichte. In H. Haag, B.G. Strauß & S. Heinze (Red.), *Theorie- und Themenfelder der Sportwissenschaft* (82-93). Schorndorf.

Langenfeld, H. (1992). Sport History: Fundamental Aspects. In H. Haag, O. Grupe & A. Kirsch (Eds.), *Sport Science in Germany. An Interdisciplinary Anthology* (423-438). Berlin.

Lawson, H. A. (1988). Physical Education and the Reform of Undergraduate Education. *Quest*, 40, 12-32.

Lenk, H. & Lüschen, G. (1976). Wissenschaftstheoretische Probleme der Sozialpsychologie des Sports. *Sportwissenschaft*, 2, 121-143.

Lenk, H. (1983). Sportphilosophie. In P. Röthig (Red.), *Sportwissenschaftliches Lexikon*. (282-283). Schorndorf.

Letzelter, M. (1978). *Trainingsgrundlagen*. Reinbek.

Lieber, H.-J. (1988). Wissenschaftstheoretische Reflexionen zur Sportwissenschaft. *Sportwissenschaft*, 2, 125-136.

Lienert, G.A. (1969). *Testaufbau und Testanalyse*. Weinheim.

Lindquist, E.F. (1953). *Design and Analysis of Experiments in Psychology and Education*. Boston.

Lorenzen, P. & Schwemmer, O. (1975). *Konstruktive Logik, Ethik und Wissenschaftstheorie*. Mannheim.

Lowe, B., Kanin, D.B. & Strenk, A. (Eds.). (1978). *Sport and International Relations*. Champaign.

Loy, J.W. & Harris, J.C. (Eds.). (1990). Body Culture. *Quest*, 2.

Martin, D. (1992). Training Science: Technique Training - An Aspect of Training Theory. In H. Haag, O. Grupe & A. Kirsch (Eds.), *Sport Science in Germany. An Interdisciplinary Anthology* (241-262). Berlin.

Mattausch, W.D. (1973). Zu einigen Problemen der begrifflichen Fixierung der konditionellen und koordinativen Fähigkeiten. *Theorie und Praxis der Körperkultur*, 9, 849-856.

Mayring, P. (1985). *Qualitative Inhaltsanalyse*. Weinheim.

Mechling, H. (1984). Bewegungswissenschaft. In K. Carl u.a., *Handbuch Sport*. (83-134). Düsseldorf.

Mechling, H. (1989). Leistung und Leistungsfähigkeit im Sport. In H. Haag, B.G. Strauß & S. Heinze (Red.), *Theorie- und Themenfelder der Sportwissenschaft* (230-251). Schorndorf.

Mechling, K. & Roth, K. (1992). Movement Theory: Motor Behavior. In H. Haag, O. Grupe & A. Kirsch (Eds.), *Sport Science in Germany. An Interdisciplinary Anthology* (201-222). Berlin.

Meinberg, E. (1979a). *Erziehungswissenschaft und Sportpädagogik. Analysen zum Theorieverständnis von Erziehungswissenschaft und Sportpädagogik*. St. Augustin.

Meinberg, E. (1979b). Handlungsforschung als sportpädagogisches Problem. *Sportwissenschaft*, 1, 29-51.

Meinberg, E. (1981a). Das ungelöste Konstitutionsproblem der Sportwissenschaft. *Sportwissenschaft*, 4, 406-419.

Meinberg, E. (1981b). *Sportpädagogik. Konzepte und Perspektiven*. Stuttgart.

Meinberg, E. (1984). *Hauptprobleme der Sportpädagogik. Eine Einführung*. Darmstadt.

Meinberg, E. (1987). Zum Ansatz einer verstehend-beschreibenden Sportpädagogik. In W. Brehm & D. Kurz (Red.), *Forschungskonzepte in der Sportpädagogik*. dvs-Protokolle Nr. 28. (37-56). Clausthal-Zellerfeld.

Meinel, K. & Schnabel, G. (1987). *Bewegungslehre - Sportmotorik*. Berlin.

Mester, J. (1988). *Diagnostik von Wahrnehmung und Koordination im Sport*. Schorndorf.

Meusel, H. (1976). *Einführung in die Sportpädagogik*. München.

Morehouse, C.A. & Stull, A. (1975). *Statistical Principles and Procedures with Applicationfor Physical Education*. Philadelphia.

Morland, R.B. (1973). The Philosophic Method of Research. In H.W. Hubbard (Ed.), *Research Methods in Health, Physical Education, and Recreation*. (305-321). Washington D.C.

Mummendey, H.D. (1987). *Die Fragebogen-Methode*. Göttingen.

NAPEHE (Ed.). (1976). Graduate Study in Physical Education. *Quest, Monograph 25, Columbus.*

Nitsch, J.R. (1989). Die Verantwortung des Sportwissenschaftlers. Gedanken zur Berufsethik. *Brennpunkte der Sportwissenschaft*, 3, 54-71.

Nitsch, J. (1992). Sport Psychology: Fundamental Aspects. In H. Haag, O. Grupe & A. Kirsch (Eds.), *Sport Science in Germany. An Interdisciplinary Anthology* (263-296). Berlin.

Nitsch, J.R. & Christen, J.H. (1984). Psychophysiologische Zusammenhänge im Sport: Modelle, Methoden, Modifikationsmöglichkeiten. In K. Carl u.a., *Handbuch Sport*. (565-586). Düsseldorf.

Orth, B. (1974). *Einführung in die Theorie des Messens*. Stuttgart.

Paré, C., Lirette, M., & Piéron, M. (Eds.). (1986). Research Methodology in Teaching. Physical Education and Sports. Trois-Riviéres.

Peper, D., & Christmann, E. (Hrsg.). (1987). *Zur Standortbestimmung der Sportpädagogik*. Schorndorf.

Petermann, F. (1989). *Einzelfallanalyse*. München.

Philipp, H. (1987). Die Experimentelle Methode. In K.-H. Bauersfeld (Red.), Forschungsmethoden in den sportmethodischen Wissenschaftsdisziplinen. *Wissenschaftliche Zeitschrift der DHfK*, 28, Sonderheft 3, 89-119.

Piéron, M. (1989). Pédagogie du Sport: Etüde de Processus d'Enseignement. *International Review of Education*, 1, 51-63.

Piéron, M., & Cheffers, J. (1988). *Research in Sport Pedagogy: Empirical Analytical Perspective*. Schorndorf.

Piéron, M., & Graham, G., (Eds.). (1986). *Sport Pedagogy. The 1984 Olympic Scientific Congress Proceedings*. Vol. 6. Champaign.

Pilz, G.A. (1982). *Sport und körperliche Gewalt*. Reinbek.

Pilz, G.A. (1989). Aggression/Gewalt im Sport. In H. Haag, B.G. Strauß & S. Heinze (Red.), *Theorie- und Themenfelder der Sportwissenschaft* (326-344). Schorndorf.

Pooley, J., & Pooley, C.A. (Eds.). (1982). *Proceedings of the Second International Seminar on Comparative Physical Education and Sport*. Halifax.

Popper, K. (1935). *Logik der Forschung*. Tübingen.

Preising, W. (1984). Sportpädagogik. In K. Carl u.a., *Handbuch Sport*. (23-62). Düsseldorf.

Rapp, G. & Schoder, G. (Hrsg.). (1977). *Motorische Testverfahren*. Suttgart.

Reischle, K. & Spikermann, M. (1992). Sport Biomechanics: Purpose-Oriented Biomechanical Analysis of Swimming Technique. In H. Haag, O. Grupe & A. Kirsch (Eds.), *Sport Science in Germany. An Interdisciplinary Anthology* (163-190). Berlin.

Reschke, E. (1989). Rechtswissenschaft und Sport - Sportrecht. In H. Haag, B.G. Strauß & S. Heinze (Red.), *Theorie- und Themenfelder der Sportwissenschaft* (160-173). Schorndorf.

Rieder, H. & Schmidt, I. (1980). Grundlagen der Sportmethodik. In O. Grupe (Hrsg.), *Einführung in die Theorie der Leibeserziehung und des Sports.* (267-315). Schorndorf.

Rieder, H. & Huber, G. (1989). Sport mit "Sondergruppen". In H. Haag, B.G. Strauß & S. Heinze (Red.), *Theorie- und Themenfelder der Sportwissenschaft* (302-315). Schorndorf.

Rittner, V. (1974). Zur Konstitutionsproblematik der Sportwissenschaft. *Sportwissenschaft,* 4, 357-371.

Rittner, V. (1984). Körper und Sport. In K. Carl u.a., *Handbuch Sport.* (607-620). Düsseldorf.

Rittner, V., Mrazek, J. & Lammersdorf, M. (1984). Zur Entwicklung und zu fortbildungsschwerpunkten der Sportsoziologie. In DSLV (Hrsg.), *Trendberichte aus der Sportwissenschaft.* (48-61). Schorndorf.

Rose, D. A. (1986). Is there a Discipline of Physical Education? *Quest,* 38, 1-21.

Roskam, F. (1983). Sportstätten. In P. Röthig (Red.), *Sportwissenschaftliches Lexikon.* (362-369). Schorndorf.

Roskam, F. (1989). Technik-orientierte Wissenschaften und Sport - Übungsstätten/Geräte. In H. Haag, B.G. Strauß & S. Heinze (Red.), *Theorie- und Themenfelder der Sportwissenschaft* (174-183). Schorndorf.

Rost, J. (1988). *Quantitative und qualitative probabilistische Testtheorie.* Bern.

Rost, R. (1992). Sports Medicine: The Significance of Sport for Health in the FRG. Exemplified by Primary and Secondary Prevention of Coronary Heart Disease. In H. Haag, O. Grupe & A. Kirsch (Eds.), *Sport Science in Germany. An Interdisciplinary Anthology* (119-146). Berlin.

Roth, K.-D. (1982). *Strukturanalyse koordinativer Fähigkeiten.* Bad Homburg.

Röthig, P. (Red.). (1983). *Sportwissenschaftliches Lexikon.* (6. Auflage 1992). Schorndorf.

Röthig, P. (1983a). Rhythmik/Rhythmus. In P. Röthig (Red.), *Sportwissenschaftliches Lexikon.* (302-303). Schorndorf.

Röthig, P. (1983b). Förderunterricht. In P. Röthig (Red.), *Sportwissenschaftliches Lexikon.* (136). Schorndorf.

Röthig, P. (1989). Musik und Bewegung. In H. Haag, B.G. Strauß & S. Heinze (Red.), *Theorie- und Themenfelder der Sportwissenschaft* (252-261). Schorndorf.

Sabo, D. (1993). Sport Sociology. *Sport Science Revue,* 1.

Safrit, M. (1990). *Introduction to Measurement in Physical Education and Exercise Science*. St. Louis.

Safrit, M.J. & Wood, T.M. (1989). *Measurement Concepts in Physical Education and Exercise Science*. Champaign.

Sarris, V. (1990a). *Methodologische Grundlagen der Experimentalpsychologie*. 1: Erkenntnisgewinnung und Methodik. München.

Sarris, V. (1990b). *Methodologische Grundlagen der Experimentalpsychologie*. 2: Versuchsplanung und Stadien des psychologischen Experiments. München.

Scheuerl, H. (Hrsg.). (1975). *Theorien des Spiels*. Weinheim/Basel.

Schilling, G. (1992). Sport Psychology. *Sport Science Revue*, 2.

Schlicht, W. (1988). *Einzelfallanalysen im Hochleistungssport*. Schorndorf.

Schmitz, J. (1966). Das Problem einer "Wissenschaft" der Leibesübungen oder des Sports. *Die Leibeserziehung, 4*, 118-127. Auch in Ausschuß Deutscher Leibeserzieher (Hrsg.) *Zum Begriff der Bewegung*. (67-87). Schorndorf.

Schmitz, J.N. (1978/79). *Allgemeine Grundlagen der Sportpädagogik. Grundbegriffe - Problemfeld - Zielproblematik*. Schorndorf.

Schmitz, J.N. (1980). Fachdidaktische Grundlagen zum Sportunterricht und zur Leibeserziehung. In O. Grupe (Hrsg.), *Einführung in die Theorie der Leibeserziehung und des Sports*. (244-266). Schorndorf.

Schmitz, N. (1983). Sportdokumentation. In P. Röthig (Red.), *Sportwissenschaftliches Lexikon*. (108-109). Schorndorf.

Schnabel, G. (1987). Charakteristik der sportmethodischen Forschung und ihrer Methoden. In K.-H. Bauersfeld (Red.), Forschungsmethoden in den sportmethodischen Wissenschaftsdisziplinen. *Wissenschaftliche Zeitschrift der DHfK*, 28, Sonderheft 3, 49-62.

Schnabel, G., Gutewort, W., Hirtz, P. & Klimpel, P. (1987). Methoden zur Gewinnung empirischen Wissens. In K.-H. Bauersfeld (Red.), Forschungsmethoden in den sportmethodischen Wissenschaftsdisziplinen. *Wissenschaftliche Zeitschrift der DHfK*, 28, Sonderheft 3, 181-230.

Schnädelbach, H. (1989). Positivismus. In H. Seiffert & G. Radnitzky (Hrsg.). *Handlexikon zur Wissenschaftstheorie*. (52-58). München.

Schwenkmezger, P. & Rieder, H. (1992). Sport Psychology: Examples of Current Research. In H. Haag, O. Grupe & A. Kirsch (Eds.), *Sport Science in Germany. An Interdisciplinary Anthology* (297-328). Berlin.

Seifart, H. (1989). Sportpublizistik. In H. Haag, B.G. Strauß & S. Heinze (Red.), *Theorie- und Themenfelder der Sportwissenschaft* (316-325). Schorndorf.

Seiffert, H. (1983-1985). *Einführung in die Wissenschaftstheorie* Bd. 1 und 2. München.

Seiffert, H. (1989). Theorie. In H. Seiffert & G. Radnitzky (Hrsg.), *Handlexikon zur Wissenschaftstheorie*. (368-369). München.

Seiffert, H. & Radnitzky, G. (Hrsg.). (1989). *Handlexikon der Wissenschaftstheorie*. München.

Shepard, R.J. (1992). Exercise Physiology. *Sport Science Review*, 1.

Siedentop, D. & O'Sullivan, M. (Eds.). (1992). Secondary School Physical Education. *Quest*, 3.

Sieger, W. (1965a). Theorie der Körperkultur, methodologische Grundlagen. *Körpererziehung*, 8/9, 476-483.

Sieger, W. (1965b). Wissenschaftstheoretische Probleme der Terminologiearbeit. *Leibesübungen/Leibeserziehung* 6, 14-18.

Sieger, W. (1965c). Zur Grundlegung einer Theorie der Körperkultur. *Wissenschaftliche Zeitschrift der Deutschen Hochschule für Körperkultur*, 2, 79-90.

Sieger, W. (1968). Theorie der Körperkultur als Wissenschaftsdisziplin (eine Diskussionsgrundlage). *Wissenschaftliche Zeitschrift der Deutschen Hochschule für Körperkultur*, 2, 53-71.

Simons, H. (1984). Sportpsychologie. In K. Carl u.a., *Handbuch Sport*. (165-192). Düsseldorf.

Simri, U. (Ed.). (1979). *Proceedings of the First International Seminar on Comparative Physical Education and Sport*. Wingate, Israel.

Singer, R. & Ungerer-Röhrich, U. (1983). Alterssport. In P. Röthig (Red.), *Sportwissenschaftliches Lexikon*. (22-23). Schorndorf.

Singer R. & Willimczik, K. (Hrsg.). (1985). *Grundkurs Datenerhebung* 2. Ahrensburg.

Sixtl, F. (1967). *Meßmethoden der Psychologie*. Weinheim.

Sneed, J.D. (1971). The Logical Structure of Mathematical Physics. Dordrecht.

Standeven, T., Hardman, K. & Fisher, D. (Eds.). (1991). *Sport for All into the 90's*. Comparative Physical Education and Sport. Volume 7. Aachen.

Stegmüller, W. (1969, 1970, 1973, 1974). *Probleme und Resultate der Wissenschaftstheorie und Analytischen Philosophie*. Bd. I-IV. Berlin.

Steiner, H. (1984). Motivation im Schul-, Vereins- und Freizeitsport. In K. Carl u.a., *Handbuch Sport*. (535-564). Düsseldorf.

Stemmler, R. (1980). *Statistische Methoden im Sport*. Berlin.

Stemmler, R. (1987). Formen der graphischen Ergebnisdarstellung. In K.-H. Bauersfeld (Red.), Forschungsmethoden in den sportmethodischen Wissenschaftsdisziplinen. *Wissenschaftliche Zeitschrift der DHfK*, 28, Sonderheft 3, 249-296.

Storf, V. (1984). Wettkampfsysteme in Schule und Verein. In K. Carl u.a., *Handbuch Sport*. (877-916). Düsseldorf.

Strauß, B.G. (1990). Ausgewählte Literatur zur Forschungsmethodologie. In H. Haag & K. Hein (Red.), *Informationswege zur Theorie und Praxis des Sports*. (433-453). Schorndorf.

Strauß, B. G. & Haag, H. (1994). *Forschungsmethoden - Untersuchungspläne - Techniken der Datenerhebung in der Sportwissenschaft. Forschungsmethodologische Grundlagen*. Schorndorf.

Stützle, M. (1983). Aggression. In P. Röthig (Red.), *Sportwissenschaftliches Lexikon*. (16-18). Schorndorf.

Thomas, J.R. & Gill, D.L. (Eds.). Ethics in the Study of Physical Activity. *Quest*, 1.

Thomas, J.R. & Nelson, J.K. (1990). *Research Methods in Physical Activity*. Champaign.

Toulmin, S. (1981). *Voraussicht und Verstehen*. Frankfurt/M.

Trogsch, F. (1962). Forschungsmethoden und Forschungsmittel auf dem Gebiet von Körperkultur und Sport. *Theorie und Praxis der Körperkultur, 3*, 245-251.

Trogsch, F. (1973). Entwicklung der Sportwissenschaft und ihre Bedeutung für Dokumentation und Information. *Theorie und Praxis der Körperkultur, 12*, 1079-1085.

Trogsch, F. (1975). Wissenschaftsdisziplinen, Wissenschaftsentwicklung und interdisziplinäre Forschung. *Wissenschaftliche Zeitschrift der Deutschen Hochschule für Körperkultur, 1/2*, 143-149.

Ungerer, D. (1977). *Zur Theorie des sensomotorischen Lernens*. Schorndorf.

Ungerer, D. & Daugs, R. (1980). Bewegungslehre - Unter besonderer Berücksichtigung der Sensomotorik. In O. Grupe (Hrsg.), *Einführung in die Theorie der Leibeserziehung und des Sports*. (142-182). Schorndorf.

Ungerer-Röhrich, U. & Singer, R. (1984). Zur Entwicklung und zu Forschungsschwerpunkten der Sportpsychologie. In DSLV (Hrsg.), *Trendberichte aus der Sportwissenschaft*. (5-19). Schorndorf.

Urhausen, A. & Kindermann, W. (1992). Exercise Physiology: Performance Diagnostics and Training Control. In H. Haag, O. Grupe & A. Kirsch (Eds.), *Sport Science in Germany. An Interdisciplinary Anthology* (69-104). Berlin.

Watson, G.G. (1986). Sportwissenschaft in der postindustriellen Gesellschaft: einige Richtlinien für die Zukunft. *Sportwissenschaft, 3*, 245-267.

Widmer, K. (1977). *Sportpädagogok. Prolegomena zur theoretischen Begründung der Sportpädagogik als Wissenschaft*. Schorndorf.

Willimczik, K. (1968). *Wissenschaftstheoretische Aspekte einer Sportwissenschaft*. Frankfurt.

Willimczik, K. (1975). *Grundkurs Statistik*. Frankfurt.

Willimczik, K. (Hrsg.). (1979). *Wissenschaftstheoretische Beiträge zur Sportwissenschaft* (Scientific Theory Problems of Sport Science). Schorndorf.

Willimczik, K. (1980). Der Entwicklungsstand der sportwissenschaftlichen Wissenschaftstheorie. Eine internationale vergleichende Analyse. *Sportwissenschaft*, 4, 337-359.

Willimczik, K. (1983). *Grundkurs Datenerhebung 1*. Ahrensburg.

Willimczik, K. (1985). Interdisziplinäre Sportwissenschaft - Forderungen an ein erstarrtes Konzept. *Sportwissenschaft*, 1, 9-32.

Willimczik, K. (1987). Sportwissenschaft/Wissenschaftstheorie. In H. Eberspächer (Hrsg.), *Handlexikon Sportwissenschaft* (Handbook Sport Science), 443-467. Reinbek.

Willimczik, K. (1989). (Irr-)wege einer Ethik der Sportwissenschaft, *Spectrum der Sportwissenschaft*, 1, 5-25.

Willimczik, K. (1992). Interdisciplinary Sport Science - A Science in Search of its Identity. In H. Haag, O. Grupe & A. Kirsch (Eds.), *Sport Science in Germany. An Interdisciplinary Anthology*. (7-36). Berlin.

Willimczik, K. & Roth, K. (1983). *Bewegungslehre*. Reinbek.

Winer, B.J. (1971). *Statistical Principles in Experimental Design*. Tokio.

Winkler, J. (1988). *Das Ehrenamt*. Schorndorf.

Wolf, N. (1984). Die strukturelle und inhaltliche Entwicklung des Schulsports von 1945 bis zur Gegenwart. In K. Carl u.a., *Handbuch Sport*. (795-820). Düsseldorf.

Wonneberger, G. (1954). Zum Artikel von M. Zeuner: Die Frage der Körpererziehung als Wissenschaft. *Theorie und Praxis der Körperkultur*, 12, 1029-1033.

Wonneberger, G. (1965). Westdeutsche Leibeserziehung und Sportwissenschaft im Dienste und Schatten der Aufrüstung (1956-1961). *Wissenschaftliche Zeitschrift der Deutschen Hochschule für Körperkultur*, 2, 113-120.

Wonneberger, G. (1968). Zur historischen Position der Sportwissenschaft in der DDR. *Beiheft zur Zeitschrift Theorie und Praxis der Körperkultur*, 117-120.

Woodman, L. (1993). Coaching Science. *Sport Science Revue*, 2.

Zimmer, H. & Klimpel, P. (1987). Theoretisch-logische Methoden. In K.-H. Bauersfeld (Red.), Forschungsmethoden in den sportmethodischen Wissenschaftsdisziplinen. *Wissenschaftliche Zeitschrift der DHfK*, 28, Sonderheft 3, 49-62.

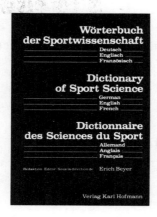

Dictionary of Sport Science

German, English, French
2nd edition 1992

Editor Professor Dr. Erich Beyer

The expansion of scholarly research and the progressive specialization into scholarly sub-fields of the relatively young sport science has, as it is the case in other fields of scholarly research, too contributed to the developmental tendency to an intensified differentiation of the technical terminology. The newer a field of scholarly research is, the less set its terminology. This is especially true of sport science, and this is the reason why it is difficult to communicate not only within one's own linguistic boundaries, but also in international cooperative efforts. To diminish such difficulties, to make the foreign scholarly literature accessible, and thus to further international cooperative work, an international team of about 140 scholars from Germany, USA, Great Britain, France, and Luxemburg have prepared this trilingual "Dictionary of Sport Science. German — English — French". 915 trilingual definitions of technical terms are classified synoptically and arranged in alphabetic order. International experts provided relevant annotations to indicate differing usages in the different linguistic domains. Clearly arranged indices help to find the terms.

The dictionary tries to provide greater clarity in dealing with sport science terminology and to stimulate a comparative scholarly consideration of the field. It is certainly a valuable source of information for scholars, teachers, and students.

Size 6,7 × 9,4 inch, 772 pages, ISBN 3-7780-3502-9
The dictionary costs US $ 47.— including surface postage, if you wish delivery by airmail it costs US $ 57.—.

Please order with check:

Verlag Karl Hofmann · P.O. Box 1360 · D-73603 Schorndorf